SIMON & SCHUSTER CROSSWORD PUZZLE BOOK

Series 229

*New challenges in the original series,
containing 50 never-before-published crosswords*

Edited by JOHN M. SAMSON

A Fireside Book
Published by Simon & Schuster
New York   London   Toronto   Sydney

FIRESIDE
Rockefeller Center
1230 Avenue of the Americas
New York, NY 10020

For information about special discounts for bulk purchases,
please contact Simon & Schuster Special Sales:
1-800-456-6798 or business@simonandschuster.com

Designed by Sam Bellotto Jr.

Manufactured in the United States of America

10 9 8 7 6 5 4 3

ISBN 0-7432-2269-5
ISBN 978-0-7432-2269-3

COMPLETE ANSWERS WILL BE FOUND AT THE BACK.

FOREWORD

Here's a different kind of puzzle from the inventive mind of Harvey Estes.

QUEEN ANNE'S LACE PUZZLE

Like the bloom of the Queen Anne's lace flower, this puzzle has a single dark spot. There is one black square in the puzzle that falls inside the gray area. Your job is to solve the puzzle and figure out where the black square belongs. The clues are given in order but are not numbered.

ACROSS

Battery size
Crockett's "Miami Vice" partner
Wild and crazy guys
Bhutto, for one
Morning coffee
Part of a Pound poem
Depression era prog.
Hollywood hopeful
Chose
Placido's "that"

DOWN

Boom box insert
It may cover UCLA and LSU
Let up
Started liking
Went across
Noted pyramid builders
Hagar the Horrible's hound
Small chest muscle?
Roth plan

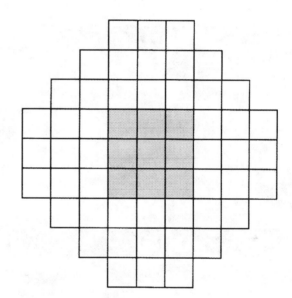

The Margaret Award winner is ROLLER COASTER by Nancy Nicholson Joline.

JOHN M. SAMSON

IF YOU ENJOY OUR PUZZLES, HERE'S MORE TO EXPLORE.

Simon & Schuster has been publishing outstanding crossword puzzle books every year since 1924—a grand tradition that continues into the twenty-first century.

The world's first and longest-running crossword series continues its tradition of all brand-new and totally original puzzles, constructed by top experts in the field. Editor John M. Samson promises another year of prime cruciverbal wizardry that will keep your brow furrowed and your mind spinning.

So get out your pens or pencils, sharpen your wits, and get ready for months of brain-teasing fun!

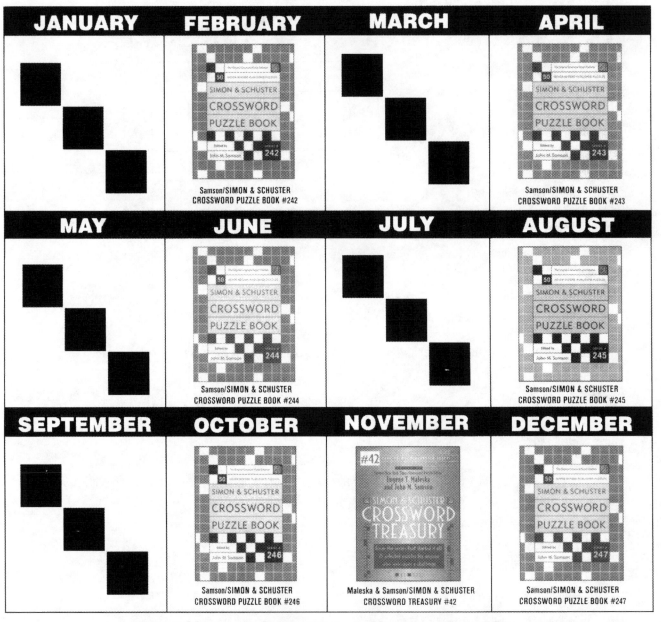

JANUARY

FEBRUARY
Samson/SIMON & SCHUSTER
CROSSWORD PUZZLE BOOK #242

MARCH

APRIL
Samson/SIMON & SCHUSTER
CROSSWORD PUZZLE BOOK #243

MAY

JUNE
Samson/SIMON & SCHUSTER
CROSSWORD PUZZLE BOOK #244

JULY

AUGUST
Samson/SIMON & SCHUSTER
CROSSWORD PUZZLE BOOK #245

SEPTEMBER

OCTOBER
Samson/SIMON & SCHUSTER
CROSSWORD PUZZLE BOOK #246

NOVEMBER
Maleska & Samson/SIMON & SCHUSTER
CROSSWORD TREASURY #42

DECEMBER
Samson/SIMON & SCHUSTER
CROSSWORD PUZZLE BOOK #247

**For Simon & Schuster's online crosswords,
visit us at www.simonsays.com.**

1 FALSE STARTS   by Patrick Jordan
"On your mark, get set, . . . oops!"

ACROSS

1 Not as good
6 Seat on Scout
12 Feline line
16 Jacob's father
17 Irish home fries?
18 Seascape tint
19 Like Mercury?
21 Ladder crosspiece
22 Big time
23 Some finals
24 Comfort
26 Storklike waders
29 Takes out of text?
30 Easily educated
33 Tones
34 Sports artist Neiman
36 Be a cultivator/ carpenter?
39 Derek and Diddley
42 "Don't move a muscle!"
43 Navigator Ericson
44 Paul Bunyan tales, e.g.
45 Send into ecstasy
46 Skating competition
48 Like strychnine
49 Barracks array
50 Stinging comment
51 Combat zone
52 Give a whirl
53 Gopher's countenance?
56 Oboist Craxton
57 The Auld Sod
58 Ruff, to Dennis the Menace
59 For a special purpose
62 Humiliate
64 Takes care of
66 Runs without moving
68 Minded moppets
71 1/63,360 mile
72 Retrieve a silver-gray drawing?
76 "Off the Court" author
77 Soap scent
78 British Columbia neighbor
79 Poverty
80 City near Santa Rosa
81 Yam, for one

DOWN

1 Anniversary celebrant
2 Capital on a fjord
3 Barbecue spoiler
4 Lose firmness
5 Audible comeback
6 Castro Convertible
7 Do away with
8 Smeltery waste
9 Telegraphic signal
10 Leader of the Rebs
11 Termini
12 His sole friend was Scrooge
13 Share the value of
14 Perfume quantity
15 Salary
20 Three in one
25 Garbage scow trait
27 He chases "that wascally wabbit"
28 Weigh-station trucks
30 Produce a change in
31 Masseur's milieu
32 Accord
33 "Purple ___": Hendrix
35 Ump's counterpart
37 2000 Subway Series team
38 Defendant's need
39 Cereal POP
40 Camden Yards mascot
41 Confidential
44 Nessie's natatorium
46 Wore a groove in the rug
47 Glacial ridge
48 Harry Potter, for one
50 Ostracize
51 Excels
53 Almanac tidbit
54 "Cannonball Run" director
55 Happy song syllables
56 Gave a ribbing to
59 Resident E of the Urals
60 Slow on the uptake
61 Anne in "Auggie Rose"
63 Prefix for burst
65 Does in, to Tony Soprano
67 School recital segment
68 Use a bayonet
69 Cavity indicator
70 God with a goat-drawn chariot
73 "All Over the World" band
74 Freight unit
75 University URL suffix

2 DIPTERA by Jack Hammond
The title is explained at 39 Down.

ACROSS

1 Beetle relative
7 Dense
11 First Family of 1910
16 Business end of a stamen
17 Photojournalist Yamasaki
18 Tiff
19 City of NW Venezuela
20 What has lorgnettes and 39 Down?
22 ___ SHRDLU
23 The guys at BBD&O
24 Acclivity
25 Persuasion
27 Glass smoker
29 Like Jack Kerouac
32 ___ candy
34 Wound
36 New Zealand warrior
38 Direct
40 Type size
45 What a drover does
46 Gracie in "Honolulu"
47 Deity at Thebes
48 Reputed inventor of rugby
49 Islet
50 Legal right
51 Stead
52 Rathskeller item
54 Reference daggers
55 Little Iodine, for one
57 Intermediate, to the judge
58 Pole that's tossed
59 Oppressed Japanese
61 Limited competition
63 Proceeds
64 Egg white
68 Medieval stringed instrument
70 Some are wild
71 Like a PT Cruiser
76 "Stay tuned for ___ forecast"
80 What has a long line and 39 Down?
82 Rabbit's foot, e.g.
83 ___ a million
84 The Chinese call it Shamo
85 Ovum
86 Lots
87 "The Girl with the Hatbox" star
88 Vivacious wit

DOWN

1 Clustered jewel setting
2 Sculptor's study: Abbr.
3 French city once known as Briovera
4 What has 55,601 seats and 39 Down?
5 Nest in the Rockies
6 Medium state
7 Ancient Greek promenade
8 Lt. Columbo's outfit
9 City near Mount Timpanogos
10 Eroded
11 Thyrotropin, for short
12 Squash choice
13 Pomona's realm
14 Armor plate
15 "Inside the Third Reich" author
21 ABM part
26 Basketball coach VanDerveer
28 "___ little teapot . . ."
29 Manhattan munchies
30 Like vitamin C
31 Ornamental plant
33 Empathizes
34 ___ of the minds
35 Aleta's first-born
37 ___ Hunley (Civil War sub)
39 Diptera
41 What has gum wrappers and 39 Down?
42 Marine monad
43 John
44 Complete
50 "Bones" is one
52 Like a bairn
53 Approach
56 À la
60 What has a forked tail and 39 Down?
62 Vichyssoise, e.g.
64 Attempt
65 "Mule Train" singer
66 Befuddled
67 Kazakhstan river
69 Torquemada
72 Cackleberries
73 Hurry
74 Loungewear item
75 Aesir bigwig
77 Oriole, but not a Cardinal
78 Tibetan mystery
79 Cancel a dele
81 Little-used PC key

3 LAZYBONES   by Gayle Dean

73 Across has been called the greatest American humorist since Mark Twain.

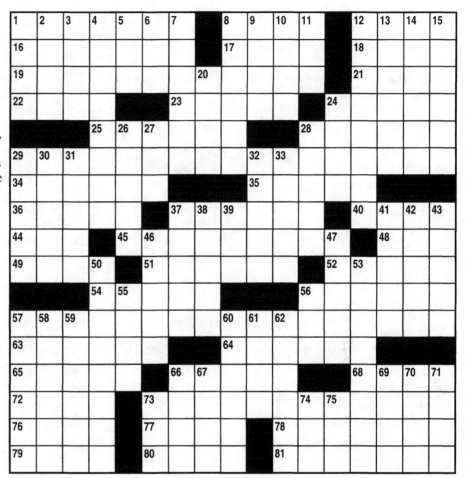

ACROSS

1 Shaded promenade
8 Economist Smith
12 Vocal range
16 Sound measure
17 Dinner beverage in Naples
18 It's for the birds
19 **Start of a quote**
21 "Consuelo" novelist
22 Mary ___ Lincoln
23 Pains
24 Cleric's residence
25 Those in a mess?
28 Retinues
29 **Quote continued**
34 Eagerly
35 Stomach
36 Lariat
37 Circus tent
40 Shankar of the sitar
44 Coll. course
45 **Quote continued**
48 Ewen in "Pearl Harbor"
49 Postlude to a kiss?
51 Stupid
52 Piano-key wood
54 More feeble
56 Word in an Orwell title
57 **End of quote**
63 "___ We Stand"
64 Mute
65 Monopoly collections
66 Land of a black falcon
68 Dubliner's land
72 Chomp down on
73 **Author of quote**
76 River through Opole
77 Medicinal plant
78 Meriting
79 Youngsters
80 Ignis fatuus
81 Holey cheeses

DOWN

1 Mine entrance
2 Mother of Apollo
3 Aqua fortis, e.g.
4 Wrongdoings
5 Slacken
6 Astrologer to Elizabeth I
7 Tennis player Gibson
8 Against
9 Mysophobiac's fear
10 Hill dwellers?
11 Jane Smiley bestseller
12 Assaulter
13 Shanty
14 Past, present, and future
15 Most curious
20 Belmont race
24 "Star Trek" con man
26 Distribute
27 Plaything
28 Shore bird
29 Some are "hallowed"
30 Help
31 Distant prospect
32 Takes out on the town
33 "Heavens ___!"
37 City in Shinar
38 Short presentation
39 Black wildebeest
41 Lemon asset
42 Mercenary
43 Short pastoral poem
46 Found a target by radar
47 "The Life of Jesus" author
50 Serving pieces
53 Marsh birds
55 Manhattan has 12
56 Summer quencher
57 European flatfish
58 Lake near Syracuse
59 Tipped off
60 Catching some z's
61 Adapts
62 Makes happy
66 Bamako's country
67 Israeli novelist Oz
69 Bird associated with Thoth
70 Russo in "Outbreak"
71 Units of work
73 Jabber
74 Command to Dobbin
75 William Tell's canton

4 "WADDLE THEY SING NEXT?"   by Richard Silvestri

If it looks like a duck, walks like a duck . . .

ACROSS

1 Rodan's land
6 Atlantic City game
11 Spry
16 Bring down
17 Moroccan capital
18 Church halls
19 Trio tripled
20 ___ which way
21 "Halt!" to a salt
22 Jay's announcer
23 "Awake and Sing" playwright
24 Wound up
25 Ducky Everly Brothers tune?
30 "Don't bet ___!"
31 Won going away
34 "Disorganized Crime" star
36 Not holding water
38 Locomotive section
40 Half of Hispaniola
41 ___ d'Or (Cannes award)
42 Source of harm
43 Ducky Righteous Brothers tune?
47 Proceeds
48 Holiday songs
49 Pays to play
50 "Season of Glass" singer
51 Love to pieces
52 Stray Cats guitarist
54 A Musketeer
56 "___ yellow ribbon . . ."
57 Ducky Honeycombs tune?
64 Llama's habitat
67 With us
68 It fits in a lock
69 Looks like a letch
70 Do penance
71 Didn't move a muscle
73 Classic Western
74 Parlor piece
75 "Barnaby Jones" star
76 Got rid of the squeaks
77 Dillies
78 Handle effectively

DOWN

1 "Rocky Horror Show" heroine
2 Residence
3 Gift from China
4 Enzyme ending
5 Jersey cager
6 College units
7 Four-star reviews
8 Helps in a heist
9 Do a grammar chore
10 Oink pen
11 Gray area?
12 Threw in the towel
13 Terrible tsar
14 Word of comparison
15 Borgia in-law
23 Tom Joad, for one
26 Abhor
27 ___.Arie
28 Stage presentation
29 Rube
32 Two-handed card game
33 Ire
34 Frozen ___ daiquiri
35 Ancient Roman official
36 Tureen accessory
37 "Desire Under the ___"
39 Turkish governors
40 Science-fiction award
41 Duke or earl
42 Battle cry
44 Small person
45 Lariat feature
46 Down the road
51 Got together
52 Victory Gallop's jockey
53 Green land
55 Brian of "I Confess"
58 Enjoy home cooking
59 Tom T. Hall song
60 1000 fils
61 Spur
62 Eye shade
63 General drift
64 To boot
65 Radar's drink
66 Buy and sell
70 Foofaraw
71 Handful
72 Stat for Sosa

"I'M ON THE OUTS WITH . . ." by Harvey Estes
. . . a painter, three thespians, and a singer!

ACROSS

1 Agrees
6 "Life Goes On" character
11 Jezebel
16 Bridge call, informally
17 Soap Box Derby site
18 Blown away
19 Sports figures
20 Investigation aids
21 Harpo Marx et al.
22 Fauvist painter
24 "Poet in New York" poet
25 Where 2 is better than 1
26 Sigma preceders
27 "The Scarlet Letter" actress
29 Pressing need?
30 Nonprofessional org.
31 Bellum opposite
32 "Spooky" singer Dennis
33 Diaper powder
34 Tizzy
36 Hindu wonder-worker
37 Magician's aid
39 No specific one
40 Graff of "Mr. Belvedere"
41 "La Bamba" actor
45 Gabrielle in "Body Snatchers"
49 "Teaching ___ Tingle" (1999)
50 Drunk as a skunk
55 "The Job" star
56 Half step from B
59 "I see," facetiously
60 Its business is growing
61 Mil. morale booster
62 Kerouac's "Big ___"
63 Little of comedy
64 "Kate & Allie" actress
66 Skirt length
67 Mom-and-pop org.
68 Hackneyed
69 "Both Sides Now" singer
72 "Foyer of the Dance" painter

73 "Head of Iris" sculptor
74 Esther of "Good Times"
75 Probe
76 It happens
77 Pungent veggie
78 Low poker pair
79 Copy made from a stencil
80 "While My Guitar Gently ___": Beatles

DOWN

1 Good name for a kidder
2 Indispens- able
3 Tall, skinny guy
4 No way out?
5 NL 1998 MVP
6 "South Pacific" song
7 Barely manages
8 Lacking class
9 Part of ASCII
10 T or F, on exams
11 Words mouthed to a TV camera
12 Tiger Paw tire
13 "Chain Gang" singer
14 Prepares for testimony
15 "Owner of a Lonely Heart" band
23 Nasdaq blocks
24 Barker or Luthor
27 "Splash" star Hannah
28 French 101 verb
29 Tag antagonists
31 "La Bamba" actress
35 Like Antarctic weather
36 Hand with an attitude
38 Interesting introduction

42 Build up
43 Estimator's phrase
44 Lively wit
45 Soviet sub class
46 Pale ale?
47 Auburn's avian mascot
48 Camping-gear store
51 Headset part
52 Whopper junior?
53 Cut into thin slices
54 Homer Simpson's exclamation
57 Utterly absurd
58 Meet by chance
61 http://www.simon-says.com, e.g.
65 Moves carefully
66 Dell add-on
69 Rocker Jon Bon ___
70 Heckle or Jeckle
71 Zoom, for one
72 Banned bug killer
73 "Up" is their album

REMEMBER WHEN . . .   by Norman Wizer
. . . you were sitting at your desk in English class?

ACROSS

1 Take shape
5 Clobber
9 Hilltops
14 Ta-ta, in Toledo
16 Promise, for one
17 January gem
18 **Start of a quip**
21 Balkan state
22 Friendly, in Firenze
23 Comdr. superior
24 Part of road sign
26 Biographical suffix
27 Dakota Indian
28 **Quip continued**
34 Conifer
35 Yang's partner
36 Haus wife
37 Happening
40 Six pointers
42 Red type?
45 **Quip continued**
50 Subway gate
51 Place to get fit
52 Up and about
53 Contender
55 CIA forerunner
57 East Anglia cathedral
58 **Quip continued**
64 Guy from the hood
65 Sales terms
66 Maegashira's sport
67 Italian bread?
69 Compulsion
71 Two make a Spanish quart
75 **End of quip**
78 Ed Wynn's son
79 "Bring It On Home ___": Cooke
80 Montmartre's ___ Coeur
81 Lamb product
82 In a little while
83 Not now

DOWN

1 White canine
2 Repute
3 High ground
4 Religious songs
5 Wetland
6 Inter ___
7 Jack-tar
8 Watering down
9 Chum
10 Snow of the NBA
11 Capital of Turkey
12 Guardian
13 Express
15 Nobel Prize winner Nelly
17 Guck
19 "Mister Roberts" director
20 Mantilla
25 Link
28 Is
29 Vertical
30 Snowboarding stunt
31 Barbara Bonney solo
32 Miraculous food
33 Bollixes up
34 Candlemas mo.
38 Unsophisticated
39 Tiny Tim's daughter
41 Help plea
43 Religious rituals
44 Old womanish
46 He sees the future
47 On top of
48 Flings
49 Juiceless
54 Sum up
56 Dumb compress?
58 Threesomes
59 Lots
60 "Apassionata" is one
61 Cofounder of GE
62 Islamic rulers
63 Word on diet products
64 Amanda of "Gunsmoke"
68 Alcohol lamp
69 Brando movie (with "The")
70 Air, in combinations
72 Part of RIT
73 4,840 square yards
74 Anna who played "Nana"
76 Barn bed
77 Compose

7 CONGREGATIONAL MUSIC   by Bud Gillis
You won't find these songs in any hymnal.

ACROSS

1 Central point
6 Eighty-six
11 Tombo, on Maui
15 Saddam subject
16 One of a corporeal quintet
17 How shrimp may be served
19 Any "M*A*S*H" episode
20 Legally invalidate
21 Rho successor
22 Hayley Mills tune from "The Parent Trap"
25 Area in front of a goalie
27 Most alluring
28 Sty "Hi!"
29 Joplin creation
32 Emulate an FHA official
33 Early Apr. workaholic
36 Misery
37 Causes 36 Across to
39 Plumber's concern
40 Neonate's sock
41 Better half
43 1966 hit by The Happenings
48 They're cut by cutups
49 Narcotic sedative
50 "Talking Vietnam" singer
51 Thrusting swords
53 Roy Jones Jr. target
56 Word ignored by alphabetizers
57 Gulf adjoining Somalia
59 May hrs. in Memphis
60 "Three Generations" pianist
61 Re matrimony
64 Like some tabloids
66 Judy Garland classic
70 Reef component
71 Prom queen's wear
72 Aerial-shot source
75 Catch with a loop
76 " 'Til next time!"
77 Townie
78 Skirt cut
79 Successful trio?
80 Sappho's Muse

DOWN

1 Early space station
2 Hotheadedness
3 Love in "Lethal Weapon"
4 Bubble and ___
5 Delicate shades
6 Deer sir
7 Road-hazard marker
8 Puny pups
9 With keenness
10 Sweet William et al.
11 Run ___ (deteriorate)
12 Army subdivisions
13 Moulin Rouge, for one
14 Highest point
18 Listener's loan
23 No laughing matter
24 Gibson ingredient
25 "How now?" addressee
26 Carnival hot spot
30 ___ spumante
31 FBI guys
34 Present, as a problem
35 Maturation agent
37 Place for a buzzer
38 "The Boy Who Cried Wolf" author
39 "Here boy!"
40 Tourney passes
41 From ___ finish
42 Schoolmarm's favorites
43 Person from Paisley
44 Individually
45 Short-lived
46 Like some poems or proportions
47 Having colorful patches
51 Go with another name
52 Liar in Acts
53 Mrs. Roger Rabbit
54 Campfire evidence
55 "Tell Me ___": The Belmonts
57 Small bay of the sea
58 Never say this
60 One with a fitting job
62 1980s video game giant
63 Exams for would-be attys.
65 100 kopecks
66 Sajak and Trebek, e.g.
67 Oceans of time
68 Send a coon climbing
69 Metallica drummer Ulrich
73 It may say "Welcome!"
74 Jedi Master ___ Kloon

8 HOLLYWOOD WEDDINGS   by Edgar R. Fontaine
An all-new version of the Celebrity Match Game.

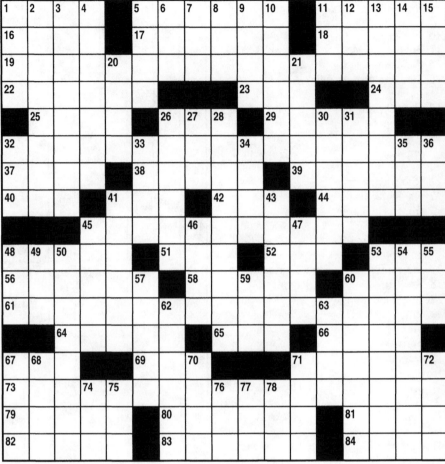

ACROSS

1 Palindromic address
5 Obliquely
11 Go with the flow
16 Peace Nobelist Myrdal
17 Baltic state
18 Battle royal
19 Hollywood wedding?
22 Private bosses
23 Byron's daughter Lovelace
24 Blighted tree
25 Palooza of comics
26 ___ Paulo
29 "We have met the ___ . . .": Pogo
32 Hollywood wedding?
37 Binary digits
38 Dowager
39 Evasion of duty
40 Four-poster
41 Zing
42 Ryan in "Restoration"
44 Home on the range?
45 Framboises, to a French chef
48 Exclude
51 However
52 It makes Burt burst?
53 Mr. Bojangles' dance
56 Prophet
58 One without a cause?
60 Loesser's "If I Were a ___"
61 Hollywood wedding?
64 It's full of hot air
65 Seashell seller?
66 Ailments
67 Little legume
69 Miss Piggy, reflexively
71 Extended family
73 Hollywood wedding?
79 Family car
80 Spookier
81 Bannister's distance
82 Experiments
83 Yankee on a pony
84 Pound sound

DOWN

1 Shiny wheels
2 Irving Berlin song
3 Did a so-so job?
4 Mutilates
5 "For pity's sake!"
6 ___ Quentin
7 Inc., in the UK
8 Clark's "Mogambo" costar
9 Singer Simone
10 Bicycle built for two
11 Jack Horner's last words
12 Rocker Shannon
13 Ooola's husband
14 Banana split?
15 Carter had one
20 At hand
21 Frenzied
26 Sharp-tongued
27 Foot up
28 Mileage measurers
30 Playacts
31 Broods
32 Carl Reiner's son
33 Inspires reverence
34 Aquarius' vessel
35 Montreal street
36 Hiver's opposite
41 Steamroll
43 Balkan state
45 CART car
46 Baffin Bay hazard
47 Seagirt land
48 Pursue relentlessly
49 Heir homophone
50 Quick fixes
53 Bend the truth
54 Start of a Shakespeare title
55 Twist together
57 Purgative
59 Scrooge expletive
60 "Sunrise at Campobello" star
62 Hummed
63 Thoughtful
67 Attention getter
68 Sang-Ki Lee's sword
70 Logical beginning?
71 Memo opener
72 Ooze
74 Kit ___ bar
75 Doubles in tennis?
76 Sis's sib
77 Free (of)
78 Sushi fish

9 "THE FUGITIVES" by Fred Jackson III
A terse thriller from a Pontiac puzzler.

ACROSS

1 Comic singer in an opera
6 Rearward on a ship
11 "Get lost!"
16 Blacksmith's wear
17 Tippy craft
18 Grafton's "N Is for ___"
19 Dallas hockey team
20 Stone monument
21 Stirred
22 CHAPTER ONE: MANHUNT!
24 CHAPTER TWO: CROSSFIRE!
26 Like winter soccer
27 "I Am Sam" star
28 Being, in Latin class
29 A type of grass
30 "Bet-a-million" Gates, notably
32 Kitchen test
36 Tennis term
37 Enter la-la land
41 The best is first
42 Yorick's skull, for one
44 McQ in "McQ"
45 Miss-named
46 Jejune
47 Country legend Acuff
48 Ayres or Archer
49 Hawk
50 The old shell game
51 Dick Smothers' brother
52 This pinto can't be ridden
53 Nimbus
54 Anastasia in "Anastasia"
56 Suit or tai
57 McDermott of "The Practice"
58 Harry Potter's protection
60 Supermodel Landry
62 In a jiffy
65 It can be petty
66 Composite picture

71 CHAPTER THREE: TRAPPED!
73 CHAPTER FOUR: REHABILI- TATION
74 Bandleader married to Ava
75 Split asunder
77 Nice cap
78 "Seamarks" poet
79 Largest antelope
80 Emerge
81 Worship
82 Carter of "Wonder Woman"
83 Say "Nyah, nyah, nyah . . ."

DOWN

1 Robeson and Pinza
2 Muckraker Sinclair
3 The old shell game
4 Pass on
5 One kind of drilling
6 Point the finger at
7 Sheepish sounds
8 Violinist Kavafian
9 Lose
10 Mortise inserts
11 Fly in the ointment
12 Trail hand
13 Olympic gear company
14 " . . . evil, to ___ a king": Sam.–1 12:19
15 "With Reagan" memoirist
23 Give it a shot
25 X, in algebra
27 Tune-up
31 A very lo-o-o-ong time

32 Lords in "Cry-Baby"
33 Baseball's "Hammerin' Hank"
34 "Every Breath You Take" singer
35 "Hearts in Atlantis" psychic
36 She played Asta's owner
38 Shaq
39 "The Most Happy ___": Loesser
40 Jailbird
42 Kind of placement
43 Nog's father
44 Meadow
48 A sign of summer
49 Shrinking
51 Figure skater Goebel
52 Avon spa

55 More willowy
56 How kids fingerpaint
57 Archie's nickname for Edith
59 Hardy partner
60 Daughter of Christopher Plummer
61 Bud's bud
62 Milan opera house
63 Pair-___ shell
64 Overhead
67 At that place
68 Ancient Roman courts
69 Jeans name
70 Floral Lauder perfume
72 At this place
73 Incline
76 Moving vehicle

10 JAMMIES SESSION   by Patrick Jordan
Solve this one while listening to Brahms' Lullaby.

ACROSS

1 Mexican munchie
5 Automaton
10 Autumn chore
16 Almost shut
17 Defendant's out
18 Like your thumbprint
19 Make manageable
20 Mortise go-with
21 Obtain
22 Downsize
23 Sleepy toddler's request
25 Wedding-cake features
27 Startling shout
28 A driver is employed here
29 Rhone tributary
31 Allow to catch up
35 Outfitted
36 Sleepy toddler's request
41 In need of ibuprofen
42 Target-practice facility
43 "The Unity of India" author
44 Shad product
45 Part of a USMC slogan
46 Suffers from
48 Geologic time frame
49 Be of service to
51 "Ghosts" playwright
54 Curve-billed wader
55 Sleepy toddler's request
58 Pacific predator
59 Sign on a teen's door
60 Ermine, in summer
61 Nile nipper
64 Form a colloid
65 Like most people
67 Sleepy toddler's request
72 "Senses Working Overtime" band
75 Add to a heap
76 Unsaid, but understood
77 Cornell of Cornell U.
78 To a degree
79 Try too hard for a Tony
80 Idle
81 Lipton rival
82 France's patron saint
83 Display dejection

DOWN

1 Londoner's "Later!"
2 Trojan War commander
3 Culminated
4 Tram filler
5 Hanna-Barbera reptile Wally
6 Dairy-case array
7 "Swedish Nightingale" Jenny
8 Black, to a bard
9 Lightweight motorcycle
10 Hasten away
11 Work without ___ (be daring)
12 Thrill
13 "Take this job and . . . !"
14 "M*A*S*H" extra
15 Gaggle members
23 Beaver Cleaver's expletive
24 Attend
26 Brickyard of racing
29 Egyptian beetle
30 Recessed dining area
31 Earn a gold medal
32 Director Lee
33 Holds the deed to
34 1980s sitcom star Charlotte
36 "Forgot About ___": Eminem
37 Like omophagic food
38 Sparky Lyle book
39 Beethoven's Third
40 Charges
45 Float like a butterfly
46 Pronoun for a ship
47 Whatever amount
50 "If ___ all the same to you . . ."
51 Set apart
52 A/C measure
53 Mayberry's Otis, for one
54 Scintilla
56 Fuchsin
57 Got a gander at
60 RSVP component
61 Cheney's DOD successor
62 "Goosebumps" author
63 Strains orange juice
65 Seaside town in "Jaws"
66 Appeases fully
68 Awesome act
69 Word or warn starter
70 Entry-blank datum
71 Clickable symbol
73 U-shaped drainpipe piece
74 Java, to Jacques
77 Street shader

11 MANY THINGS by Richard Silvestri

Our test solvers had many good things to say about this one.

ACROSS

1 Elton John song
6 Nursery-rhyme diner
11 Welfare payments
16 Architect Jones
17 Kind of football
18 Bridget Riley's genre
19 Attack from all sides
20 Free-for-all
21 The brainy bunch
22 New York Indians
23 Lena in "Ignition"
24 Three-ring thing
25 Many sales?
28 What's more
29 X-ray look-alike
30 Sign of nerves
33 "Joe Palooka" cartoonist
38 Split to unite
41 Cake from corn
42 Cross the threshold
43 Length times width
44 Hot issue?
45 Many sporting events?
50 Lawn-equipment brand
51 Zaragoza's river
52 Silly
53 Sunday closing?
54 Spooky
56 Smart and Smiley
57 Was ahead
58 NBA Hall-of-Famer Unseld
59 Subj. for immigrants
61 Many floor coverings?
69 Detroit problem
72 China setting?
73 Let happen
74 Out in the open
75 In any way
76 Defunct alliance
77 Parsonage
78 Had a weakness for
79 Cookout spot
80 Primed the pot
81 Wampum
82 Hard to scale

DOWN

1 Defame in print
2 Ano opener
3 Something paid
4 Double curves
5 False
6 Pago Pago person
7 Introductory piece
8 Dig find
9 With regard to
10 Menlo Park monogram
11 Part of A.D.
12 Begins the bidding
13 Hit the beach
14 Hebrides dialect
15 Hollywood Boulevard sight
24 Of the north
26 A long way
27 Drive forward
30 One and all
31 Cook up
32 Discontinues
33 Gala
34 1040 entry
35 Put away
36 Long-billed bird
37 Prior to, to Prior
39 Garage charge
40 Man-mouse linkage
41 The Spruce Goose, e.g.
46 "Black Beauty" author
47 Needing to diet
48 Calendar abbr.
49 Band booking
55 Dirtied
56 In the style of
58 Faltered in the heat
60 Parboils
61 Do tense work?
62 "Socrate" composer
63 Honshu city
64 Sings like Satchmo
65 Fold in cloth
66 Overjoy
67 Fields of comedy
68 Dive
69 Alitalia stop
70 Dando or Hunter
71 Red coin?
75 Mass robe

12 WHAT PRICE GLORY? by Sam Bellotto Jr.
How does one become the world's alltime best-selling author? (answer below)

ACROSS

1 Filled tortilla
5 Island goose
9 Water color
13 Made backwards?
17 Director Avakian
18 In ___ (stuck)
19 Oscar-winning Hanks role
20 Register ringer
21 **Start of a Stephen King observation**
25 Hide from sensors
26 Multitude
27 Where to "send your camel to bed"
28 They even things up
30 Prefix with ate
31 David in "A.I."
34 **More of observation**
38 ___ Dhabi
39 Inclined
40 Cash-and-carry company
41 Key contraction
44 Puffs up
47 ". . . round the ___ oak tree"
49 Crossword compound
50 Petty or Eastwood
51 Lumpy in "Leave It To Beaver"
54 Songlike
56 **More of observation**
61 Affliction
62 Stage name
63 Questionable
64 Part of N.W.T.
67 Latin god
68 Tips one's hat
72 Bilbao bear
73 NYPD superlative
75 "Stillmatic" rapper
77 U.N. labor org.
78 **More of observation**
83 "You ___ Beautiful": Cocker
84 Wednesday after Mardi Gras
85 Worked in a winery
86 Pfizer rival
89 Basilica area
91 Where Jell-O was born
92 **End of observation**
98 Saloon stock
99 Cargill in "Up Pompeii"
100 Slime
101 Where Hades seized Persephone
102 Fattest president
103 Catch one's breath
104 "The Running Man" director
105 Horror writer Koontz

DOWN

1 Psych exam
2 Macaw genus
3 Isaac Newton invention
4 Frittata
5 Boris Badenov's friend
6 Composer Satie
7 Greek consonants
8 Aquatints
9 Mellows
10 Rubaiyat stanza
11 He makes home calls
12 Boulle character
13 It may be real
14 Putin's assents
15 Kirghizian range
16 Macy's department
22 Spitsbergen loc.
23 Mount Sinai
24 Word on Jamie Salé's cap
28 Russian royal
29 1944 Nobelist physicist
30 Churchill's successor
32 "Just answer yes ___!"
33 Greek dessert
35 Left at sea?
36 Fussed with feathers
37 "Amen, ___ be none.": Shak.
42 "The Sound of Music" baroness
43 Wind up a film
45 Razzle-dazzle
46 Skeleton, for one
48 Give the green light to
50 Buddy
52 Whenever
53 XXVI × IV
55 Bark
56 Paintballs, e.g.
57 New Mexico art colony
58 Standoffish
59 Steep
60 From the hip
65 Med. specialists
66 Salutes twice
69 Senate majority
70 Chimney duct
71 Auctioneer's last word
73 Splits in two
74 Kenya's largest park
76 Separated
79 Xenophobic
80 Have no ___ (dislike)
81 Reddish-brown gem
82 Squirreled away
86 Cartoonist Drucker
87 "A Day Without Rain" singer
88 Ring around an atoll
90 On the surface
91 Goof off
93 Director Lee
94 Grazing area
95 Lowe's item
96 Cytoplasmic acid
97 Sen. Brownback's st.

13 BLOCK PARTY   by Frank A. Longo

A wide-open grid design with thematic interlock and not one three-letter word!

ACROSS

1 Puzzle type
7 Terra ___
12 Frightens
18 Become decent
19 Root with a Nobel
20 Tie type
21 Copies Cousteau
22 Excessively excited
23 Rock salt
24 Mild to the max
25 It may be blessed
26 Eastern Christian
27 Makes out
28 Japanese-Canadian
29 Liszt's Lola
30 Draw the line
32 Greenhouse of a different color?
34 Unlike this clue
36 In a bit
37 Four blocks
48 Tony winner Tessie
49 Aquarium buildup
50 Conrad in "East Lynne"
51 Really regretting
52 Topic of discourse
53 Pay the penalty
54 Castle of dance
55 Acrobat's apparel
57 Barber's leather band
58 Three blocks
61 Mitigate
62 Yugoslavia's Broz
63 Man of "1000 Voices"
68 Place for an anchor
74 Hardened
75 Leatherneck neckwear
79 Stretch runner
80 Mrs. Rocky Balboa
81 Recent, in Rotterdam
82 Tenant
83 Tad
84 Evan of the Lemonheads
85 "___ In New York": Duke
86 Capital of Amazonas
87 Año beginner
88 Rubber-necked
89 Northumbria founders
90 Like most movies
91 Tears up

DOWN

1 Court cutup
2 If
3 Constant complainers
4 Amen!
5 Put-down artist
6 The Met's Manhattan locale
7 Three blocks
8 King of Norway (995–1000)
9 Pitchfork feature
10 Your, to Friends
11 Three blocks
12 "Carnaval" composer
13 Anticipate
14 Garage job
15 Strong sedative
16 Sweathogs' mentor
17 Bashful friend?
31 It comes in ears
33 Libertine
35 Out
36 Unlikely to reconsider
37 Containing element #5
38 Loansharking
39 College in Greenville, PA
40 Italian painter ___ di Pepo
41 Five-time PGA winner
42 Mountain feature
43 Grind together
44 Starbucks offering
45 Attic area
46 Madrileño's title
47 JFK's "Why England ___ "
55 Heart-healthy
56 It may be blind
59 Doornail's state?
60 Not quite bourgeois
63 Foul odor
64 Mr. Tambo
65 Siren skill
66 Nuptial
67 Hanseatic ___
69 Clue collector
70 Share the lead
71 Free from doubt
72 Looked like
73 They may be bucked
76 Jazz singer Krall
77 Article of belief
78 Poet Lorde

14 "DUH!" by Elizabeth C. Gorski
"At times it's good to be kept in the dark." — Dracula

ACROSS

1 Nile reptiles
5 Current unit
11 "Amazing!"
18 Pac-10 team
19 Tore, of yore
20 Eisenhower Center site
21 Primatologist Fossey
22 Two-footed critters
23 Daytime performance
24 **Start of a quip**
26 "Et voila!"
27 Liability for a music major
28 Recounted
30 "Harvest" singer DiFranco
32 Decorated anew
35 "Just ___!"
37 Take the bait
39 "___ for Lawless": Grafton
42 "I owe you ___ of gratitude"
44 Illegal phone-carrier act
46 "Christmas Comes But ___"
49 Bath break?
50 Domain
51 Dr.'s order
53 **More of quip**
61 Fire-breathing monster
62 Doppler ___
63 All-stars
68 Sound investments?
71 UK communiqué
72 Passport feature
73 Part of AARP
74 Wake-up call
75 Soprano Te Kanawa
77 Mother Cabrini, e.g.
80 London's ___ Gardens
81 Daly and Robbins
83 Ankle bone
87 Graves in "Mission: Impossible"
92 **End of quip**
95 "What a perfect gift!"
96 Make lovable
97 Pot plant
98 She plays Ally on TV
99 Tiger's position
100 Manitoba Indian
101 Loops
102 Type of salad
103 In ___ (actually)

DOWN

1 Visit from the tax man
2 "Forbidden Planet" genre
3 Unpretentious
4 "The Woman Rebel" founder
5 Tree-planting time
6 Rabin's predecessor
7 "Oh, My ___"
8 Happening
9 Soldier of 1776
10 Collectible Fords
11 Nightingale trademark
12 Construction beam
13 Sky box?
14 New Haven collegians
15 Fought like cats and dogs
16 Mano a mano
17 Barely visible
25 Negative of 54 Down
29 Outlaws
31 Joan Cusack's "Mr. Wrong" role
33 Chemical ending
34 "Face the music!"
36 In the vicinity
37 Medical plan, briefly
38 UN fiscal agency
39 Petty of "Point Break"
40 Designer de la Fressange
41 Sign of healing
43 "Academic Overture" composer
45 Letters on a letter
47 Wright wing
48 "___ missing something?"
49 Laundry-list item?
52 "Later!"
54 Sean Connery, for one
55 Shell oysters
56 Refrain syllable
57 Kentucky Derby month
58 Baltic tributary
59 Hard to find
60 Once, once
63 Neighbor of Mont.
64 "Frasier" script
65 All together
66 "All Things Considered" ntwk.
67 Not worth a tinker's ___
69 Bake-sale gp.
70 Hung around
72 Olive stuffing
76 "Now humble as the ___ mulberry": Shak.
78 "Ixnay!"
79 Medium's state
82 Bubbly drinks
84 Boxes, but not cartons
85 After, in Arles
86 School of Paris
88 No good at all
89 ___ majesté
90 "A River Runs Through It" star
91 Gas sellers, for short
93 Signature pieces?
94 Collar fabric
95 Water cooler

15 MIXED BAG   by Joel Kaplow
A delightful blend of originality, wit, and challenge.

ACROSS

1 Child's card game
7 "True Grit" setting?
13 "Get lost!"
18 National park in Maine
19 Band type
20 Alb covering
21 LUTE TRY
24 McFadden of "Star Trek"
25 Granola bit
26 Appear to be
27 Spelling or 10 Down
28 She raised Cain
29 Very, in music
31 Songstress Flack
33 Like most volcanoes
36 Having more info
39 Psychic Geller
40 "Jack Sprat could ___ . . ."
42 ". . . he had a cow ___"
46 FADED CROCKS
52 Army abodes
53 Crazy bird?
54 Dit's counterpart
55 Moisten flax
56 C Sicily peaks
57 Precious pebbles
60 South African language
61 Pecs' partners
62 Tyler who is 54?
63 ___ the finish
64 Arles aunt
65 MINI ACHES
70 Ashcan School artist
71 Uptight
72 Merkel in "42nd Street"
73 Eights event
76 Earthshaking
80 NASA's Earth observer
83 Virgin or Blue Note
86 Yolanda's year
87 "There oughta be ___!"
88 Part of a thespian?
91 Moo
92 Main points
94 SHAMED GANG

98 "___ bleu!"
99 "Mission: Impossible" star
100 Colorful cat
101 Birth
102 Suit you can really dig?
103 Sings like the birdies sing

DOWN

1 Estimated
2 Page size
3 Mrs. Sprat, vis-à-vis Jack
4 Bordeaux brainstorm
5 "Dear ___ . . ."
6 "Shallow ___" (2001)
7 Bubbly beverages
8 "West Side Story" girl
9 "___ a Liar" Bee Gees
10 "Bliss" singer
11 Not done well
12 Ticks off
13 "___ of a gun!": Joey Bishop
14 Standards
15 Stubble remover
16 Wide awake
17 They spread the word
22 "Father of the Modern Hot-Air Balloon"
23 Mine, to Monet
29 Color to dye for?
30 On purpose
32 Driftwood?
34 Civilian togs
35 Woofs
37 It's in the env.
38 Hop Sing's pan
40 Ancient Dead Sea region
41 Fervent fussings
43 Gofer's gig

44 Think up
45 Horse handler
46 See 12 Down
47 Like some teas
48 Paris-based UN org.
49 Professeur's pupil
50 "___ Billie Joe": Gentry
51 So preceders
57 Whitney's wonder
58 Burden
59 Hemsley of the NFL
60 "___ Bulba"
62 Some are parallel
64 "Cactus Flower" heroine
66 Gateway components
67 Communications giant
68 Brother of Osiris
69 Petrol
74 Duds

75 Coral isles
76 Emulates Betsy Ross
77 Niblick's bagmate
78 Altogether
79 Carl Sagan series
80 Cow catcher
81 Highway to Fairbanks
82 They make horse collars
84 Rootless plants
85 Phony
89 Get over it
90 Houdini interviewer Ferber
92 Nibble
93 Wait for the green light
95 Encountered at the opera?
96 Jay's voice male?
97 Tread the boards

16 PLEONASMS by Manny Nosowsky
Six excellent pleonasms are waiting to be uncovered.

ACROSS
1 "Excellent!"
8 12th-century poet/algebraist
12 Be mocking
18 Nanga Parbat locale
19 It comes with hot rolls
20 White elephant, e.g.
21 Snoop, redundantly
24 Hotbeds
25 Graffito signature
26 Puerto ___
27 Fossil fuel
28 Peril, redundantly
33 Lookout
37 Window ledge
38 "Stop" at sea
41 Grand Canyon State
42 Keep afloat
43 Way or means
44 Pitched perfectly
45 Think through
46 Made better
47 ___ Equis (Mexican beer)
48 Pechora's mountains
49 They ruin it for others
50 Careful examination, redundantly
54 Spring road hazards
57 Wrong turns
58 Get flat
61 Lets go of
62 Sotto voce call
63 Lulus
66 Smarts
67 ___ the Great (boy detective)
68 Pause on the way
69 Rockoon for weather
70 Literally "I am unwilling"
71 Poor practice
72 Urge, redundantly
75 ___-cone
77 Calls a strike
78 Standard product?
79 Inventor Nikola
84 Join forces, redundantly
89 Equally undemanding
90 Worthy Wordsworth words?
91 Maritime Territory locale
92 It had a part in the Bible
93 Hot
94 Hot ___

DOWN
1 Connate
2 Go down
3 Many ABA members
4 Close
5 What's left out
6 Start of the song "Mother"
7 Land of Isaias Afwerki
8 Few: Comb. form
9 Dallas cager, briefly
10 Distaste
11 In a fanatic way
12 Medea's jilter
13 Bridge expert Culbertson
14 See 2 Down
15 Second-longest US river
16 "A Bushel ___ Peck"
17 Kiddy litter?
22 A beaver slaps this
23 Golden Bears' school
29 Relative of -trix
30 Wont, redundantly
31 Yielded
32 In a monotone
33 Aforementioned
34 Cubic Rubik
35 Petty complaints
36 Lao-___ (Chinese philosopher)
39 Litigant
40 Spreads for drying
42 "Ruy ___": Hugo play
43 Mine, in Montréal
45 Exec. office
46 Bldg. units
48 Brings into play
49 Tallow source
50 Magician of radio days
51 Pined (for)
52 Cutlass or 98, for short
53 Move up
54 Kisser
55 Enlightened about
56 Like sprinter shoes
58 Pear-shaped instrument
59 "Like ___ not!"
60 Catch sight of
62 Defense fence
63 Slant
64 And the like
65 "Shoot"
67 Amateurs
68 Manage
70 Winsor McCay character
71 Throw in the towel
73 Bush moniker
74 Verse
75 Leonine Vickery stage role
76 It smells
80 "Qui ___-vous, Polly Magoo" (1966 French film)
81 Jahan or Pahlevi
82 ___ majesté
83 Fine subjects
85 Vegas airport code
86 Suffix for malt
87 Panhandle handle
88 Brazil singer Costa

17 HEALTHY FEE by Bernice Gordon
A humorous verse concerning a certain group practice.

ACROSS

1 Barn-door fastener
5 A bit erotic
9 Angelo's instrument
13 Rudolph of "Saturday Night Live"
17 Jerusalem's Mosque of ___
18 A weather antonym
19 Indigence
20 Keyes or King
21 Lombard lake
22 First Japanese capital
23 In the distance
24 Stone Age tool
25 **Start of a verse**
28 Fires
29 ___ in the sky
30 2000 Jamie Foxx film
31 Early space station
33 Put in the hold
37 Gain control
39 Tartish
43 Amigo of Guevara
44 Bill's partner
45 Anteros, for one
47 Maple genus
48 **More of verse**
52 Timesaver
54 Most meager
55 Take a nibble
56 "Oo ___": McCartney
57 ___ case
59 Overturn
61 Antagonist
64 Curtain ___
66 Hive loafer
71 **More of verse**
74 "America's Puppet Master"
75 Judicial decisions
76 Chiropractic org.
77 Stone marker
78 Ben Hogan rival
79 Laboring
83 Orchestrated
84 Blake Edwards film
86 "___ a little pony . . ."
87 Souchong, e.g.
88 Spouter in Sicily
91 **End of verse**
98 Ho-hum

99 Hodgepodge
100 Help a felon
101 Suit with a "reet pleat"
102 Tori Amos song
103 Ooze slowly
104 Troglodyte's home
105 Precursor to the KGB
106 Pair of draft animals
107 Dollops
108 Draw together
109 Became madder?

DOWN

1 Rinehart and Winston's partner
2 Sri Lankan nanny
3 Pundit
4 Give a poke
5 Spoiled
6 Like the griffin
7 King mackerel
8 Graduate's keepsake
9 An analgesic
10 Prove to be false
11 Doyenne du Comice, e.g.
12 Pertinent
13 Yankee cap?
14 Swimmer Popov
15 School on a 2001 stamp
16 They get in your pants?
26 Window sign
27 Patriotic soc.
32 "The Girl ___ Sunny Tennessee"
33 Health resorts
34 Nasdaq stock group
35 Lunchbox cookie
36 "Don't ___ Be Happy": McFerrin
37 Playful
38 Level, in Canada
40 Lecher's look
41 Emmy winner Ward

42 ". . . not Saturnine, as Tarquin ___": Shak.
44 Gulager in "The Virginian"
46 Gagarin's spacecraft
48 Pointed
49 Steel girders
50 Grey in "Sutter's Gold"
51 Where barnacles are removed
53 Hoagie
58 Word on a tombstone
60 Basil sauce
61 Men in black
62 "Black ___": Atherton
63 Lo!, to Caesar
65 "___ most unusual day . . ."
67 Victrola vendor
68 Parley in "Dave"

69 First name in mysteries
70 Old-time expletive
72 Not indelible
73 Food in the army
77 He crosses the line
80 Put in order
81 Shouts of excitement
82 Marietta College conf.
83 Six-line stanza
85 Promote
87 Roman coin collector?
88 Anxious
89 Nairobi ___
90 Marijuana plant?
92 Kind of collar
93 A single-malt Scotch
94 "Alligator" shirt
95 Lethargic
96 Go at an easy gait
97 Seven-card ___

18 DROPPING IN by Frank A. Longo
An unexpected visit from our Pittsburgh punster.

ACROSS

1 Llanelli's land
6 Superlatively spruce
14 Narcs, e.g.
18 Napoleon on Elba
19 "Monty Python" cast member
20 Cause for cramming
21 What's found in Greg Louganis' autobiography?
23 First name in western novels
24 Collected
25 Dundee disavowals
27 It's based in McLean, VA
28 "Pollyanna" penner Porter
29 Aardvark that bugs people?
33 "Just ___ thought!"
34 It can be corny
35 George's mother on "Seinfeld"
36 Where a pan might be?
42 Tinkered
43 Superior to
44 Yevtushenko's "Babi ___"
45 Strong-force particle
48 Singer Stratas
50 Retrovirus component
52 Conrad Siegfried's agency
53 Cat descriptor
56 Isn't right
57 Skid row headline?
60 Natalie Wood's sister
61 Filthy digs
62 Delivery on the farm
63 ___-mo
64 React to sunlight, perhaps
66 Relax
68 Young'___
70 Release, in a way
71 Tars' spars
74 One kingdom + three daughters = major tragedy?
77 Nabs in a sting
80 Chalons-___-Saône
81 Altdorf is its capital
82 Class for horse doctors?
84 "No, really, go ahead"
89 Missouri ally, once
90 Monte Rosa, e.g.
91 Haydn's "The Seasons," e.g.
92 Prefix for ester
94 What occurs when seafood buffets open?
98 In the style of, in Aquila
99 Gold medal, e.g.
100 Touch and taste, in Turin
101 Secretary
102 Necessitated
103 Cafeteria collection

DOWN

1 Shim, e.g.
2 Kind of symmetry
3 20 sols, once
4 Skater Berezhnaya
5 Woos with song
6 Rigor
7 Post's palomino
8 Pain
9 "His master's voice" co.
10 ___ for tat
11 Twin Cities suburb
12 London square
13 Teachings
14 Tasseled topper
15 "Quite so"
16 "Gigi" actress Delorme
17 Vilified
22 Irregularly notched
26 Scraps
29 Clavicle connectors
30 Rock alternative
31 1997 Bond girl
32 Merce Cunningham ballet
36 Best Actress of 1990
37 Roeper's partner
38 Pitiful
39 "Symphony No. 3" Pulitzer winner
40 Far from beneficial
41 Clapboard cry
46 He came before U
47 Baffin Bay explorer
49 Revelatory cries
51 It may follow a ques.
53 Réne Préval's purview
54 Composer Morricone
55 Host holder
58 Suffix with cell
59 Lacking focus
60 Fontanne's other half
62 Cantaloupe kin
65 Most amusingly odd
66 French auxiliary
67 Colombian coin
69 Directed a hose at
71 Tablet for 101 Across
72 France's France
73 Constitutionals
75 Peridot's mo.
76 Heep of literature
78 He cried "Ecce homo!"
79 Hungarian city
83 Bounded
85 Rena in "Keeping the Faith"
86 Silver-medalist Slutskaya
87 Bike bar
88 "___ Coy Mistress": Marvell
91 Seep
93 Hairy Himalayan
95 One with many unhappy returns?
96 "___ tu": Verdi
97 Up to the time of

19 TURF TIP by Melvin Kenworthy
Some sage advice from an Oregonian outdoorsman and lawn doctor.

ACROSS

1 Stringer support
8 Open just a tad
12 Fuse unit
18 Tom Jones, for one
19 Tommy of Broadway
20 Conqueror of Mexico
21 **Start of a turf tip**
24 Shabby
25 Hué holiday
26 Sun-dance tribe
27 Mount St. Helens outflow
28 Quartet, less one
29 Point-system writing
31 Sordid
32 Long fish
33 French affirmative
34 Clarinet in "Peter and the Wolf"
35 Deerstalker
36 Dip
39 Sprinkling
40 Hurt the most
43 Sour British brew
45 Name a ship
47 Grounds for a time-out
49 Wharton School subj.
51 Blow one's stack
52 Links lulu
53 **More of tip**
57 Development parcel
58 "What a great ride!"
59 Sphere beginning
60 Words for Nanette?
61 Faber's pencil partner
63 More lascivious
65 Curls the lip
66 Scene
68 Scurried about
72 "___ La La La Suzy": Jan & Dean
73 Jeckle's remark
74 "The Pickwick Papers" author
75 River to the English Channel
76 Ill-tempered one
78 Contrariety
80 Wags
81 Iris layer
82 Kind of pocket
83 Catcher's place?
84 Napoli resort
85 **End of tip**
90 Box the compass
91 Who or whom ender
92 Singly (with "one")
93 Like some headphones
94 Rorem and Sparks
95 Broke a promise

DOWN

1 Like a unicorn horn
2 Whistle blower
3 Involves
4 Yiddish yo-yo
5 "What will ___ think of next?"
6 Relay segment
7 Dial a wrong number, e.g.
8 Columbus on Oct.1, 1492
9 It may be poetic
10 "Harvest" singer DiFranco
11 Sequel
12 Lot measure
13 He slapped Curly
14 Church dignitaries
15 Heating cones
16 "Still Me" author
17 "Mourning Becomes Electra" husband
22 Italian bell town
23 It merged into Verizon
29 Expense itemizers
30 Murphy's claim to fame
31 Marching-band instruments
33 "Blast-off" preceder
35 "Stormy Weather" star
37 "A Boy Named Sue" singer
38 Part of n.e.s.
39 Cleaver
40 Swing at the air
41 Body politic
42 NASDAQ sector
44 Needed ibuprofen
45 B&E, for one
46 Cyd Charisse, ___ Finklea
47 High-hatters
48 "You used to come ___ o'clock. . ."
50 "We Do Our Part" org.
53 Paul Bunyan's cook
54 Butler's pursuit
55 Caen's neighbor
56 Benning or Bliss
62 Backtracker
64 Detergent of yore
66 Bern river
67 Made little of?
69 Where J.S. Bach is buried
70 Like the X-Games
71 Thirsted
73 Tear along
74 Dutch African
76 For all to see
77 He might get rubbed out
78 "___ for Peril": Grafton
79 ___-broom (woadwaxen)
80 John Walton portrayer
81 "The X-Files" transports
82 Maserati or MG
84 Highland group
86 Buffalo-Rochester dir.
87 Lexington or Park
88 Sea dog
89 Ending for Manhattan

20 MATH PROBLEM by Rich Norris
Here's a problem no one has been able to solve.

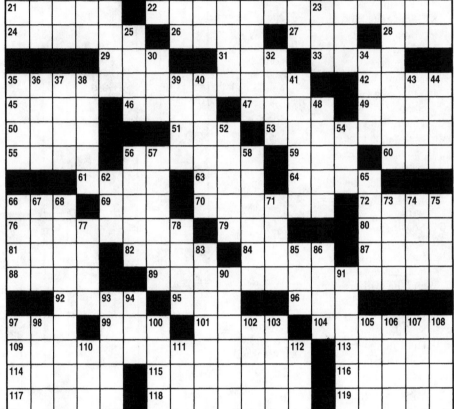

ACROSS

1 Some jabs
6 Goes over
13 Trendy mag
18 God of the Koran
19 Watts or Horowitz
20 Top of the morning?
21 S. S. Van Dine's Vance
22 **Start of a quip**
24 "Cheers" or "Frasier"
26 Car roof with removable panels
27 Join
28 Chinese cooker
29 Publisher Ballantine
31 Letter addenda
33 About
35 **More of quip**
42 "Beau Geste" novelist
45 Palm starch
46 Zenith
47 Can't do without
49 "What's ___ you?"
50 "Jabberwocky" opener
51 Mil. training academy
53 **More of quip**
55 **More of quip**
56 Toasts
59 Barley beard
60 "Great!"
61 Bank takeback, for short
63 **More of quip**
64 Go ballistic
66 Plant pouch
69 Flexible wood
70 Quint Asper, for one
72 **More of quip**
76 **More of quip**
79 Mom-and-pop gp.
80 Parting word
81 Witty Bombeck
82 Condemn
84 Rock's Mötley ___
87 Grand place (with 110-D)
88 Some spirits
89 **More of quip**
92 2000 Florida news item
95 Lennon's lady
96 Personnel datum
97 Part of NATO
99 "Smoking or ___?"
101 Durante song starter
104 Shirley Temple is one
109 **End of quip**
113 Jukebox favorite
114 Papal vestment
115 "___ Place"
116 Realizes
117 Marked areas
118 Not-so-great rating
119 Luxor tips

DOWN

1 Swimmer's regimen
2 K–12
3 Dart
4 Rash treatment
5 Odds-on favorite
6 Econ. yardstick
7 Falling-out
8 Hops dryer
9 He sleeps on his house
10 Homer, for one
11 Relative of -ites
12 Pack away
13 Barnard students
14 Switch positions
15 Snug, to a sailor
16 It's held at diners
17 Siberian city
23 PBS funder
25 Early Yucatán settler
30 Giants' gp.
32 Haggis ingredient
34 Branch branch
35 Dog star
36 En-passant capture
37 "Good grief!"
38 Basic reply?
39 Melville novel
40 Cheap tires
41 Go over again
43 The Sundance Woman
44 Prying
48 Soft
52 Batter's concern
54 Merkel of movies
56 Fail to save
57 Grovel
58 Sew
62 Looker
65 Molly in "Milk and Honey"
66 Mob ending
67 Off course
68 Own up
71 Where Prissy worked
73 Little drinks
74 Chicago's Merchandise ___
75 Ma with a cello
77 Long green
78 Area N of Piccadilly Circus
83 Priestly garb
85 Good times
86 Timea Nagy's sword
90 Copier supplies
91 Send abroad
93 Builds a pot
94 Exclamation from 10 Down
97 Whole nine yards
98 ". . . echo resounds ___ the glen": Burns
100 Nautilus captain
102 It may be tied in church
103 Looped handle
105 Stick in the fridge?
106 Mont. neighbor
107 "Aargh!"
108 Plight
110 Corrida cheer
111 Cartoon canine
112 "___ Blues": Beatles

21 MINI-MENAGERIE   by Harvey Estes
A good one for the young at heart.

ACROSS

1 Skilled in
7 Needle bearer
11 "Definitely!"
18 Surfing, perhaps
19 Jon Arbuckle's dog
20 Still on the plate
21 Young swimmer's stroke?
23 Bulkhead
24 Second sequel tag
25 Take out of context?
26 Buckeyes' school
27 "Bali ___"
28 Uno plus dos
30 Cole Porter's "___ Gigolo"
31 Short, sultry spell?
34 Flat filler
37 It gave Hope to GIs
38 Collagist Max
39 Parasol purpose
41 Linguist Chomsky
43 London gallery
45 Drink for the Green Hornet?
47 Lowers the lights
49 Gangster's gat
53 Kindergarten break?
55 Witherspoon in 60 Down
57 Compos mentis
58 Conditions
59 Small pastry?
61 J.E.B. Stuart's org.
62 Walk with weariness
64 Ma's instrument
65 Elementary school diploma?
69 Roman tragedian
71 Impend
73 Gunpowder containers
74 Quattro, for one
76 Cardinal, not an Oriole
78 End of a Garbo line
79 Daily doctor repellant
82 Flanders of "The Simpsons"
84 "My Fair Lady" lyricist
86 A little wisdom?
88 Blood-typing system
89 Wilson's predecessor
93 Bk. checker
94 Butter serving
95 Piecrust furrows
98 ___-Magnon
99 "Marathon Man" star
102 Lionel train part?
104 Walkie-talkied
105 Staff symbol
106 Used the last (of)
107 "If I Ran the Zoo" author
108 Gives the ax to
109 Church councils

DOWN

1 "Understood"
2 Studio sign
3 Blast from the past
4 Chip enhancer
5 "And giving ___ up the chimney he rose"
6 Photo start
7 Pikachu or Meowth
8 Musher's race
9 "Well done!"
10 Comics shriek
11 Fault-finder
12 Low, tied score
13 Stephen of "The Crying Game"
14 Dated
15 Donny or Marie
16 Track meet events
17 Sign up
22 Whitney and Wallach
26 Suffix with humor
29 Point of view
31 Beat with one's fists
32 Himalayan humanoid
33 Code subject
35 High-strung
36 Spotted
39 Archie's admonition to Edith
40 Tries to pick up
42 Deheat via currents
44 Big brute
45 Record problems
46 440 or 10K
48 Big-top barker
50 Add hastily
51 Like some inspections
52 Lists
54 Word by a door handle
56 Try for a fly
60 "Legally ___" (2001)
63 Handed out hands
64 Bounder
66 Middle figure
67 "Show Boat" bundle
68 Good egg
70 Feeds a line to
72 Memorable "Voice of the Yankees"
75 Viscera
77 Turns down
79 International agreement
80 Tree with catkins
81 Kilt patterns
83 ME time
85 Campus marchers
87 Rapiers
90 Blessing preceder
91 Austrian analyst
92 Wrongful acts
95 ". . . season to be jolly, ___ . . ."
96 Antony's loan request?
97 "Freeze, Fido!"
100 Strive
101 Debtor's letters
102 New Deal prog.
103 Paula Zahn's org.

22 IMAGE-MAKERS   by Sam Bellotto Jr.
An amusing aphorism from a Pulitzer Prize–winning columnist.

ACROSS

1 Biblical verb
5 2000 Senate majority whip
9 "Moulin Rouge!" director Luhrmann
12 Orrin Hatch's state flower
16 Cookie since 1912
17 Like Chewbacca
18 Bygone
19 River to the Caspian
20 **Start of a Jimmy Breslin quote**
24 Mouth of a stream
25 It's found among the reeds
26 "Doggone it!"
27 Mild expletive
29 No ifs, ___, or buts
31 "South Street" singers (with "The")
35 Charlie Parker
38 Pay-as-you-go fee?
40 "The Gods ___-begging": Handel
42 Toledo tots
43 Suffix for Campbell
44 Where Quechua is spoken
45 Friend of Zazu
47 Simulacrum
48 **More of quote**
52 Hip-related
53 Jaworksi or Panetta
54 Kyoodle
55 "Almost ___ Count": Brandy
57 Fashionable
60 Rings a bell
64 Noun suffix
66 Ignore (with "out")
68 Simone's school
69 **More of quote**
74 Cook Cajun-style
75 Shrek and Fiona
76 Balsams
77 Secret ending
78 Hammock ends
80 LeMay's WW2 outfit
81 Biggest Little City
82 Fun ending
83 IAD airport

85 "Return of the Jedi" sage
87 Ray Palmer's secret identity
89 Vigorous pull
91 Metropolitan areas
93 Gotten used to
97 **End of quote**
102 Pakistani language
103 Fireworks display?
104 Massey in "Rosalie"
105 Cafeteria item
106 Bryant on a 1997 stamp
107 Keglers' org.
108 Part of DOD
109 Hankerings

DOWN

1 Arizona Indian
2 Adam Trask's favorite son
3 Head of government?
4 Worked like a horse
5 Jean-___ Ponty of jazz
6 Guesser's words
7 Siouan, say
8 Chicken brand
9 "Tommyrot!"
10 Like Knockando
11 1998 Hopkins role
12 Slight effect
13 Great time
14 Four qts.
15 GOP center
17 Makes stationary
21 Dog toy
22 Woman's shoe
23 Make money
28 Genuity Championship site
30 Organism body
32 It's often enough
33 Theatre sign

34 IRS requirement
35 Cleft in two
36 "Cosmicomics" author Calvino
37 Fix a loose tether
39 Speedy sleds
41 Pres. Bartlet's wife
44 Clambake
45 State assemblies
46 Songwriter Wilder
49 Malicious fellow
50 Fracas
51 Glasgow and Greene
56 Godzilla's movie studio
58 Mu followers
59 Arkansas toothpick
61 Pitch to perfection
62 Michael Jackson prop
63 Donatello's home
65 Has-been horses
67 Twin Cities suburb
69 Short grand
70 James ___ Carter

71 Say the rosary
72 Win back
73 Madonna album
74 Chip in a TV camera
79 NYSE membership
81 Dregs
82 Like black corn
84 Dogg in "Bones"
86 Ancient Celtic priest
88 Switch positions
90 Protuberance
92 Pig out on this?
94 Like the dodo in 1600
95 Alaska's first governor
96 Old Tunis rulers
97 Parkay container
98 Swedish coin
99 Boise's county
100 Crossword solver's cry
101 Screenplay abbr.

23 OVERKILL by Randall J. Hartman
A clever challenger from an Escondido enigmatist.

ACROSS

1 Seance sounds
5 Stagehands
10 Rogers in "Ginger Snaps"
14 SPRR stop
17 Border
18 Visual beginning
19 Viking god
20 Hoosegow
21 Colorado necktie
22 Fumarole emission
23 ___ an ear
24 Ambulance staffer
25 Gets ready for sumo?
27 Together
28 Pedestal piece
29 EIR reviewer
30 An appositive
32 Rob of "Wayne's World"
34 Slowly burn
36 Cause havoc
38 Catch fungoes
40 Wake up
41 Understand
43 Keene sleuth
45 Vent, Krakatoa-style
47 Selects
48 London streetcar
50 Trial partner
52 Satellite of Saturn
54 Bar mitzvah and baptism
56 Appraises
58 ___ capita
59 Odin's realm
62 Columbian cat
64 To the point
66 Place for a "mute"
68 72, at Augusta
69 Vie for the break
71 "They ___ Horses, Don't They?"
73 Vena cava neighbor
74 Jack Nicholson role
76 Mystery writer's award
78 Warehouse pallet
79 McGwire's 1999 rival
82 Fire proof
84 Baldwin in "Beetlejuice"
86 Like bobruns

87 K-Pax, for one
89 Cleopatra's maid
91 Get smart
93 A ductless gland
95 Goals
97 Like Jack Benny, facetiously
100 RN association?
101 "Blast!"
103 Noted ark-itect
105 First name in mascara
106 Jose's aunt
107 Pop's pop
108 Boo-boo
110 Arthurian address
111 USNA grad.
112 Barkley's sobriquet
113 Choral group
114 Bedouin bigwig
115 "Orange Crush" band
116 Raison d'___
117 It couldn't stomach Jonah
118 Hanes products

DOWN

1 Synagogue figure
2 Circa
3 Crew neck?
4 "Dracula" author
5 Road sign
6 Road obstacles
7 Apotheosis
8 Grand objects
9 Bluebirds fly there?
10 Fungus
11 Ned Rorem opus
12 Will power?
13 Like arena football
14 Accelerate
15 Squall
16 Scorpio star
26 Rosebud, for one
31 Taxi rider
33 Dumbo's wing

35 Kook
37 Deborah of "The King and I"
39 ___ reaction
41 Sharpen a razor
42 "Witches" author Jong
44 Mink stole
46 Ahab's cabin boy
49 Country singer Tillis
51 Mayberry jail habitué
53 Domain
55 Man from U.N.C.L.E.
57 Booted
59 Burning the midnight oil?
60 Storage room
61 Primed
63 One in need of a poison pill?
65 Maharishi's exercise

67 Calendar pgs.
70 Tourmaline, e.g.
72 "Long ___ Sally"
74 Judy Jetson's mom
75 Stat. for 79 Across
77 Great Barrier ___
79 Splash
80 Traditional
81 David Spade's humor
83 Paleozoic or Mesozoic
85 Part of 100 Across
88 Frisée
90 Smack
92 Winter apple
94 Stout cousin
96 ___ Fe
98 John Denver album
99 Dirty looks
102 Pica or elite
104 Bounder
109 Ave.

24 "DO AS I SAY . . ." by Elizabeth C. Gorski
"Never practice two vices at once." — Tallulah Bankhead

ACROSS

1 Places
6 "Coffee Cantata" composer
10 Pampered one
13 "Assuming that's true . . ."
17 "Fo, fo! come ___ pin . . .": Shak.
18 Eye impolitely
19 Washoe, for one
20 "In the Still of the ___": Boyz II Men
21 Valuable viola
22 "Go and Tell Pharaoh" author
24 Cauterize
25 **Start of a Tallulah Bankhead quip**
28 Workplace protection org.
29 "How dumb can I be?"
30 July hrs.
32 Lord's Prayer opener
34 Knot-tying words
37 Right-angled annex
38 "Stand and Deliver" star
40 "When I was ___ I served . . .": G&S
42 Tenor Borgioli
44 VPI's Big conference
47 Hindu deity
48 Grasse head
49 Source of oil
51 Excellent service provider?
52 "Bye!"
54 Woven
55 Moonscape features
57 **More of quip**
61 King of England in 1035
65 Interpret
66 "___ Macabre": Saint-Saëns
71 Norwegian royal
72 Settled
76 Siouan
77 Mayberry moppet
78 Fictional wirehair
79 Andropov
80 Singer Chaka
81 Egyptian dye
83 French connections
85 "Wait just ___!"
87 ENT experts
88 Plus
89 Gets into a lather
93 Bombay butter
95 **End of quip**
101 Charlie's angel?
102 Coat a can
103 Like Ibsen
104 Rainbows
105 Yalie
106 Shade shade
107 Swell place?
108 Tibia end
109 Queue after Q
110 Golf shirts?
111 Programs, to Ed Sullivan

DOWN

1 ___ impasse (stuck)
2 "Mork & Mindy" character
3 Fancy
4 Choir section
5 Greeted (with "to")
6 Anjou's kin
7 Turkish honorific
8 Extended families
9 Jazz pianist Hancock
10 Relating to 108 Across
11 Strong glue
12 Coffee-break time
13 Part of NIH
14 Prey of owls
15 Remains until morning, say
16 Not 'neath
23 Little shot
26 Saratoga Springs artists' colony
27 Limo rider
31 Russian royals
32 ". . . and does eat ___ . . ."
33 1997 Peter Fonda role
35 Slickers
36 Long-billed bird
39 Juristic exam
41 "L.A. Law" actress
43 Egg
45 Splinter group
46 Noddy
50 January, in Mexico
53 The works
56 Help
58 Bean sprout?
59 Start of a child's rhyme
60 Voids
61 Fracas
62 Source of a cattle call
63 Ritual after a dry spell?
64 Hot spot
67 Affirmative on Columbia
68 Utmost extent
69 Fly high
70 Nights, poetically
73 "Go, go, go!"
74 Red condiment: Var.
75 "Ice Age" sabertooth
82 Suffix for polymer
84 Temporary rental
86 Casual pants
90 Web-footed mammal
91 Seed coverings
92 "New York, New York" actress
94 Snow of "Carousel"
96 Mantel piece
97 French 101 verb
98 ___ ex machina
99 "___ Her Standing There": Beatles
100 Wallet fillers
101 Acorn's lot, perhaps

25

MAGAZINE STAND   by Frank A. Longo
Eight magazines of past and present are hiding in the squares below.

ACROSS

1 Manipulated fraudulently
7 "Abie Baby" musical
11 "Abie's Irish Rose" star
14 Bistro bill
17 Come on the scene
18 All in front?
19 "Tin Cup" director Shelton
20 Skillful swinger
21 Sherman Hemsley role
24 Vinyl collectibles
25 "Way cool!"
26 Salubrious site
27 Kind of mutual fund
29 Rosco P. Coltrane's deputy
31 A, as in Aachen
33 Dry red wine, briefly
34 Plateau kin
35 Repeatedly
39 Think up
41 Llano's relative
42 .0000001 joule
43 Lying on the canvas
44 Bandleader Beneke
45 Child-care author LeShan
47 Spy Powers
50 Bubbletop, e.g.
51 Bill add-on
55 Mae West
58 Technological debut of 1946
59 Effective leveler
60 Gut reaction?
61 Regarding
62 Chinese restaurant freebie
65 You may be out of them
66 Supermodel Sastre
67 Campina ___, Brazil
68 Decompose
70 Guitarist Paul
71 Columnist Marilyn ___ Savant
72 Not in session
74 Polite denial
79 Book after Nehemiah
81 Site of John Brown's raid
84 Backbone
85 Murrelet's cousin
86 Wacko
87 2002 Olympic host cntry.
88 Supermodel, say
92 Datebook abbr.
94 Giant from Gretna
95 Lyon king?
96 Lagasse's sine qua non
99 Technique
100 Hupmobile contemporary
101 Orangutan's lack
102 Maurice's sleuth
103 Fly-___ (airshow thrillers)
104 W-2 info
105 Bones
106 Subway systems

DOWN

1 Feels like Miss Otis?
2 "This is no joke!"
3 Epcot symbol
4 Sore setter's sound
5 Halloween ammo
6 Increased in profundity
7 Rototiller alternative
8 Like some radios
9 Dirt
10 Wagner opera
11 1937 George Arliss film
12 Suite section
13 Like some news sources
14 Discusses the issue
15 Pacification
16 Outdo
22 Drew Barrymore's mom
23 Hold your horses
28 MLK, for one
30 Certain IRA
32 Burnsian turndown
36 Brief survey
37 "P Is for Peril" novelist
38 Malaria symptom
39 Dresses up in
40 Puts forth
43 Sutherland in "Dark City"
46 Takes in or lets out
48 Asserted oneself
49 USS Enterprise counselor
50 First Bond film
51 Catalogue anew
52 Riding the wave of success
53 Serious difficulty
54 Chow
56 Pachacuti, e.g.
57 Start of a Steinbeck title
63 Haing in "The Killing Fields"
64 It comes out in the wash
69 Operating at full capacity
71 Presidents, at times
73 Half a score
75 "Lend ___ Tenor": Ken Ludwig
76 Mail man?
77 "Scourge of Princes" satirist
78 Periwinkles
80 That fellow
81 Whopping
82 Like
83 Dennis' dog
85 Unlawful ignition
88 Interest, slangily
89 Doesn't waste
90 Some DVD players
91 Redolent neckwear
93 Hungary's Nagy
97 Ending for plug or play
98 Guinness suffix

26 DOUBLE VISION   by Elizabeth C. Gorski
A recent bout of diplopia inspired this twice-as-nice theme.

ACROSS

1 DDE's predecessor
4 Super serve
7 Cheshire Cat, for one
13 Set at an angle
17 Big leagues
19 C to C
20 Colima outflow
21 Like some sandals
22 Rating for a double feature?
24 Intellectual
25 "___ live and breathe!"
26 Managed
27 "Les Nuits d'___": Berlioz
28 Runs in place?
30 Baton Rouge sch.
33 Unanimously
35 Double-stitched lids?
40 ___ tree (stuck)
41 Local mail ctr.
42 Classical beginning
43 Causing goose bumps
47 Tom Thumb was under his thumb
51 J. N. Garner and H. A. Wallace
53 Greetings
55 Rainbow
56 Middle of the ocean
59 "___ dieu!"
60 Cola preference
61 Like the golfer after a double eagle?
64 Phony start
66 Before, to Byron
67 Accumulates, chemically
68 Mature
69 Nonschool diploma
70 It's a blast
71 Tolerated
75 Rat's reply
77 Discount-rack abbr.
79 Chowed down
82 Classic ref. work
83 Double up on sack time?
89 Got by
92 Go-aheads
93 Overhangs
94 Bonzo, for one
95 Slip up
97 Small low island
99 Join up
103 Rock group with double-platinum hits?
107 Embassy staffer
108 Novice
109 Lack of moral standards
110 "Don't come back!"
111 River to Kassel
112 Rumor-mongers
113 Furry friend
114 Vane dir.

DOWN

1 Start of a URL
2 Wingtip
3 ___ off (miffed)
4 "The Human Condition" author
5 High-priced
6 Curve in the road
7 Soaks up
8 Montreal university
9 Hairy Addams cousin
10 Lemon ___
11 Lasting beginning?
12 Soprano Scotto
13 Slick
14 Top-40 DJ Casey
15 "High Flying Adored" musical
16 Like Tussaud's figures
18 ___ vanilla
23 Govt. securities
25 Rush-job acronym
29 Shell food?
31 Ricky and David, to Ozzie
32 Monet's one
34 "Peer Gynt" figure
35 Butter bowl
36 New Deal prog.
37 Listening device
38 Cherished
39 Santa's greeting
44 Seattle forecast, often
45 Tick off
46 "Outer" word form
48 Zip
49 Scanned info
50 Street rumble
52 Hymn of praise
54 Prefix meaning "within"
57 Ski competition
58 Mystery writer Grafton
59 Booker T. & the ___
60 Indian not in India
61 Barcelona bravos
62 Press pass, e.g.
63 Fade away
64 Sun shade?
65 Inflatable item
69 Top-notch
70 March
72 Family man?
73 Comics cry
74 Canine doctor?
76 Cool cube
78 Greek letter
80 "___ All Laughed": Gershwin
81 Greek vowel
84 English Riviera
85 Volcanic island W of Naples
86 Guy de Maupassant story
87 Approached
88 California wild plum
89 Unglossy finish
90 Greenfly, e.g.
91 Mower maker
96 Surrealist Magritte
98 Sweetsop
100 Greta Garbo, e.g.
101 Ban
102 Beret's place
104 In favor of
105 It's not free of charge
106 Univ. clock setting
107 Nile denizen

27 DIS-LEXIA by Michael Collins

Ten celebrities have been singled out for some playful wordplay.

ACROSS

1 Half an old radio duo
5 Legal claims
10 Grabs
15 "Bummer!"
19 Baltic seaport
20 Mother Teresa's adopted home
21 "Belling the Cat" author
22 "Elephant Boy" boy
23 Singer tries to sound like Martin?
25 Actress becomes more retiring?
27 Like numbers less than ten
28 Chihuahua change
29 Be in a holding pattern
30 Thrice, in prescriptions
31 Lindsay's "The Bionic Woman" role
33 Sound of a Greek snoring?
34 "I've ___ up to my keister!"
38 Hymn title starter
40 Retain, in a way
44 John's "Grease" costar
46 Pointed screenwriter/producer?
48 Ward of "Once and Again"
49 "As ___ Dying": Faulkner
50 Vaudevillian Williams
52 Topple
54 Affection, in brief
55 Honshu honorific
56 Hollow President?
60 Bandleader Shaw
62 TV, newspapers et al.
64 Bill tack-on
65 Victimized (with "on")
66 Norton's workplace
67 Mouthless boy of comics
68 Mark up, at times
69 Had a good cry
71 Out
72 Per-hour wage
75 To any extent
76 Singer not as sharp as before?
78 Bacillus shape
79 "Come to think of it . . ."
80 Tea go-with
82 Tammany Tiger creator
83 "Waterloo" quartet
84 ___ 'Oléron, France
86 Actor who gets under your skin?
90 Nurse Ratched's employer
92 Something to stand on?
94 Having a scent
96 Long baskets
97 Be cute on a shoot
98 Furnace flame
99 "Chances ___"
101 Computing shortcuts
104 Stuff to the gills
105 Pass over
110 Politician looks beastly?
112 Actress who's used to taking the heat?
114 Lincoln Navigator and others
115 Prefix with play or act
116 "___ Irish Rose"
117 MSNBC talk host
118 Diana in "Oliver Twist"
119 Mississippi quartet
120 Lyons river
121 Give up

DOWN

1 With the bow
2 Demeanor
3 Lothario's look
4 The Shirelles' "Mama ___"
5 City on the Meuse
6 Rajiv Gandhi's mother
7 Change one's story?
8 "Winter of Artifice" author
9 ___ Tomé
10 RR crossing guards
11 Let out
12 City east of Bergen
13 Yours truly, facetiously
14 Cosmonauts
15 Gurus' abodes
16 Of the flock
17 Union leader I. W.
18 "Why not?"
24 Capone contemporary
26 Where it's at
28 Hummus holder
31 Erosion preventer
32 Pozzuolana
33 ___ cards (ESP testers)
34 Loading apparatus
35 Hajji's god
36 Persuasive newswoman?
37 Pole climber
39 Stuffed deli delicacy
40 FDR's Commerce Secretary
41 Actress who blew her lines?
42 "Dallas" matriarch
43 Did a 5K
45 Put up with
47 Good-looker
51 Abu Dhabi dignitary
53 Perch kin
56 Crown or family follower
57 Kingfisher's topper
58 Salon stuff
59 Pertinent, to lawyers
61 Caboose
63 "Momma" cartoonist Lazarus
65 Córdoba cash
67 Can't stomach
68 X-ray units
69 Having a high pH
70 ". . . thereby hangs ___": Shak.
71 Weight-and-fortune cost, once
72 Traffic-jam noise
73 ". . . ___ a fat pig"
74 Dutch exports
76 Wilderness Road blazer
77 Like some gases
81 Rail support
83 Firth of Clyde port
85 Bum out
87 Hangs around
88 Hanging around
89 "Hinky Dinky Parlay ___"
91 Canyon of comics
93 Make fast
95 Shade in
98 TV oldie "Hotel de ___"
100 Scrape up
101 Irish actress Gonne
102 Certain chorister
103 "Smokey" spotter
104 York and Bilko: Abbr.
105 Rock music's Cream, e.g.
106 "The Covered Wagon" is one
107 1960 Olympics site
108 Swaps, for one
109 In ___ (actually)
111 Add-___ (extras)
112 Bell and Rainey
113 Bygone hoops org.

There's a museum dedicated to 58 Across in Santa Rosa, California.

ACROSS

1 "Laughing Cavalier" painter
5 "I Bought Me ___": Copland
9 Taunt
14 Tailor's line
18 Obi-Wan portrayer
19 Bearded sect
20 Less loco
21 "Tiger-in-your-tank" gas
22 He feuded with Winchell
23 Parisian landlord's fee
24 Banana oil, for one
25 "Blue ___ Fly"
26 **Start of a quote**
30 "Good for Henri!"
31 Allay
32 Adam Vinatieri's asset
33 **Quote continued**
42 Med. school ordeals
43 Fruit skins
44 Côte d'Azur resort
45 Alien from Melmac
47 Mandalay Bay cubes
48 Divergences
49 Eliot character
51 Teen's sign-off
53 Like
54 Some of the President's men
55 Prove worthwhile
57 Roulette bet
58 **Source of quote (with 71-A)**
60 Pack animal
61 Send a file
63 Actor Ogilvy
64 **Quote continued**
66 Popeye's milieu
67 Went by
70 Loo label
71 **See 58 Across**
75 Gawk (at)
76 Ocean ___, WA
78 Absquatulates
80 ". . . are ___ body strong enough": Shak.
81 Hanging bandage
83 Mom's sister
84 "Dick Tracy" creator
85 Play bonspiel
86 Home Depot item
87 Leave out
89 Precinct squad
90 Arbor asset
91 **Quote continued**
96 Chiang ___, Thailand
97 Like the Kalahari
98 Tanqueray gin brand
99 **End of quote**
109 "Penguin-dancing" bird
110 Drum set
111 Peter who was Herman
112 Laundry unit
114 Tishri preceder
115 Beats (out) narrowly
116 Shows concern
117 Very fine quality
118 Say it ain't so
119 Arledge of ABC
120 The Mauve Decade et al.
121 She played Joanie

DOWN

1 Fate
2 Basque for "merry"
3 Toronto center?
4 Jot down quickly
5 AMA member
6 Film, to Roger Vadim
7 Hammett pooch
8 Diver's nightmare
9 Sleep-inducing fly
10 Island with arcane statuary
11 Entry fee of sorts
12 Crystal-gazer
13 All over the map
14 Parlor piece
15 Morales of movies
16 Yard-sale proviso
17 Lose plumage
19 Compaq Center, e.g.
27 Travails
28 Puts on the feed bag
29 Spur adjunct
33 Linen or tweed type
34 Russian cottage
35 Coaxes cattle
36 Leeds river
37 Printer's supply
38 Not alfresco
39 Feudal estate
40 Proportion
41 Skater Sokolova
42 Pindaric
46 Baretta's pet
48 Villainous folks
49 Starr and Simpson
50 Fictional governess
52 Muhammad's god
54 Avis features
55 Green strokes
56 Bothered (with)
59 Gotten up
60 "Western Star" poet
62 Bodybuilder's pride
64 Tropical rodent
65 Swiss Alpine Museum site
67 Luxurious
68 Shining
69 More foxy
71 Brunch fruit
72 Normal
73 Ladies' men
74 1947 Graziano opponent
77 "Abie Baby" musical
78 Print preference
79 "Abide With Me" playwright
82 Reached
84 High counselor?
85 Embroidery cord
88 Suffix for schlock
89 ___-a-brac
90 Explorer Hedin
92 "Please,___ human!"
93 Wet
94 Colorful tropical fish
95 Nebraska tribesmen
99 ". . . the life that late ___?": Shak.
100 Beauty spot
101 Substantive
102 Church calendar
103 "Aladdin" parrot
104 Bronx Zoo sound
105 ___ Bora, Afgh.
106 GPA D's
107 Sweet mate
108 Manhattan gypsy
113 Private room

29 ACK ME ANYTHING   by Fred Piscop
Question-marked clues have a lot in common with the title.

ACROSS

1 Prefix with liter
5 Hambletonian gaits
10 Sponge gently
15 Sticking point?
19 Admit openly
20 1998 "Psycho" star
21 Be in accord
22 Lo-cal
23 Sailing expert?
25 Scrape together
26 Tummy trouble
27 Turkish bigwig
28 It's picked out
29 Acid in wine
31 Like café donuts?
33 "42nd Street" opener
35 ___ chi
37 Cries from the sties
39 "People" composer
40 "Messiah" soloist
42 "___ Rappaport" (1996)
44 Help out, in a way
46 Unstable part of a ship?
48 Hilly region of NE France
49 Mortarboard tosser
50 Catch, western-style
51 Oblong fruit
52 Fuzz
55 Knotted
57 Slowly destroys
59 Bibliographic abbr.
60 Ad follow-up
63 Épée's lack
65 Ornate, as writing
66 "The Glass Menagerie" heroine
67 Slowly, in music
69 Straw bosses
71 Financial weekly founder
72 Pie nut
73 Parlor piece
74 George and Greg?
76 Starfleet Academy grad.
77 "Reginald" author
78 Encryption
79 At the drop of ___
81 "Boola Boola" collegian
82 Bubbly singer?
83 Musical Apple
86 Sing like Tom Waits
90 Fuel for a small Dodge?
92 Sounding a bit like Tom's pal?
94 Female hormone
96 Cartridge filler
97 Sends, in a way
98 Musical Cagney role
99 Alley denizen
101 "Bali ___"
103 March time
104 "Hold on!"
106 Art up one's sleeve?
108 Mil. force
110 Morse "E"
112 Ditch
113 Legend maker
115 Dirt farm produce?
118 River of Asia
119 Kitchen gadget
120 First name in cosmetics
121 Packard or Kaiser
122 Taboos
123 Assaults from Moe
124 Leans toward
125 Old muscle cars

DOWN

1 Stuff to be crunched
2 "Green Acres" star
3 It's the real thing
4 Parrot's cartoon cry
5 Whaler's adverb
6 Revert to 12:00, say
7 Series mo.
8 Bad thing to be behind?
9 Hospital supply
10 "Rats!"
11 "Encore!"
12 Mason City traffic?
13 Two-time loser to DDE
14 Ready to be driven
15 Ike of the O.K. Corral
16 Martin speculation?
17 Pallas
18 Garden gadget
24 Cake asset
30 Cozy corner
32 "I swear I ___ art at all": Shak.
34 Every señor has one
36 Throws a line to
38 Marked with an "X"?
40 E-mail address ending
41 Holy city?
43 M.Sgt., for one
45 Boxers and pugs
47 It's from hunger
48 Love, Italian-style
53 Hammerin' Hank
54 They're laid out
56 Coal site
57 Respected one
58 ___ Beauty apple
59 Stirrup's place
60 Run out
61 Utopian
62 Sight on the beach?
64 Cosmetic surgery on a grand scale?
65 Lot
66 Smallville's Lang
68 Clavell's "___-Jin"
70 Cultural values
71 Parental warning
73 Burns a bit
75 A zillion
78 Viet ___
80 Common chord
82 Blackmore's Lorna
83 Games partner
84 Cold storage?
85 Creole veggie
87 Dramatized
88 Predicts
89 APB broadcasters
91 Pastelist's purchases
92 Cooperstown's Wilhelm
93 Greek salad morsel
94 Big name in commercial cleaning
95 Santa Rosa's county
96 Turkic-speaking people
100 ___ show (street carnival)
102 Press mechanism
105 Bellyache
107 Telltale sign
109 City on the Skunk River
111 General ___ chicken
114 AFL partner
116 Loop initials
117 Fall back

ACROSS

1 Soldier's ID
4 Fashionably smart
8 Fifth Roman emperor
12 Bellini's "___ Diva"
17 "Dutchman" playwright Jones
19 Phnom ___
20 Finished
21 Playful mammal
22 **Start of a limerick**
25 ___ brûlée
26 Pedicure star
27 1846 Johann Galle discovery
28 Stints
29 Landed
31 Show surprise, e.g.
32 Golf shot
33 High horse?
36 Belgian town
37 Ancient Semitic fertility god
38 Prostate test
41 Time Warner partner
42 **More of limerick**
46 Hardly harsh
48 Eliel's son
49 Rhythmic cadence
50 Cut film
51 "The Tempest" spirit
53 "La Gioconda" was written for her
55 Locale of Phobos and Deimos
56 Nora in "The Thin Man"
57 **More of limerick**
60 Chevy truck
61 Bruce in "The Haunting"
62 Cube root of eight
63 "The City of New Orleans" singer
64 "Pollyanna" star
66 **More of limerick**
73 Seal
74 Spill the beans
75 Polish partner
76 Weird
77 "The Good Earth" heroine
78 Tent stakes
79 Throw ___
81 Dump a stock
82 **More of limerick**
88 Animator's frame
89 Cube root of one
90 Japanese aborigine
91 Mead
92 Ottawa center?
94 Skye slope
95 Trumpet fortissimo
97 Snake-eyes pair
98 Point-de-gaze designs
101 "We Were Soldiers" setting
103 Ball up
107 Cedar Rapids native
108 **End of limerick**
110 105 Down, e.g.
111 Acidity
112 ___ Park, Queens
113 Honshu city
114 National forest near Phoenix
115 "Love ___": Beatles
116 Bob tail?
117 Suffix for cabinet

DOWN

1 "To ___ and a bone . . .": Kipling
2 "The Volcano Lover" author
3 Gogol
4 Nav. rank
5 Cut down
6 Visceral
7 Tête topper
8 Cullen Sculpture Garden designer
9 Gala performance
10 Pape of the Met
11 Vein glory
12 With arrogance
13 Aweigh
14 Pipe part
15 Office part-timer
16 Olympian god
17 Frankenstein's workplace
18 Record label
23 Oder tributary
24 Upper Deck data
28 "Thou ___ Not" (Connick musical)
30 Hip
32 Yoo-hoos
33 "Les Visiteurs" director
34 Mystery writer Peters
35 Show off
37 Alaskan mountains
38 Pitcher Martinez
39 Rouen river
40 Pilaster
41 Asian servant
43 Shade of green
44 Clothed
45 Peep sites
47 Reporter's concern
52 English geologist (1797–1875)
54 Founded: Abbr.
55 Phobos and Deimos
56 "Atlantic City" director
58 Commencement gp.
59 Have
60 Trio in 64 Down
63 Dressed
64 Where to find La Scala
65 "___ at the office"
66 Union merged into UNITE (1995)
67 Lawsuit
68 Fall birthstone
69 Spats
70 ___-Roman wrestling
71 Exxon Valdez, e.g.
72 Farmer's locale
73 No great shakes
74 Geoffrey of fashion
78 Perfume container
80 Marquee word
83 Seaport of SE Italy
84 Brisk, musically
85 "From ___ shining . . ."
86 Taxed ones
87 Lemur relative
93 Job security
94 Canada goose
95 Two-legged support
96 Flip-chart stand
98 Torino car
99 Swoosh, e.g.
100 Cuba in "Rat Race"
101 Viva ___
102 ARM part
104 Paraphernalia
105 Wasserman of MCA
106 Queen Victoria Eugenie
108 Spray grease
109 Coal scuttle

ABSENTBEE LIST   by Nancy Nicholson Joline
When you come to 23 Across remember the title.

ACROSS

1 Treatise
6 Put on
12 Its capital is Bratislava
20 In the style of an earlier time
21 Rock salt
22 Form of bowling
23 Peachy-keen reviews?
25 Complete idiot?
26 Per ___
27 "___ by any other name . . .": Shak.
28 Period
29 Fairy-tale figure
30 See 28 across
31 Instruction on a proof
32 Polar bear's prey
35 More on edge
37 They're used
39 Disney septet
41 Eats or drinks
42 Fracas
43 Corn futures?
45 "N'est-ce ___?"
48 Try
51 December 31 word
52 Kind of mattress
53 Glint
54 "Bow wow!"
57 Piglet
59 Spain's English queen (1906-31)
61 "A Tale of Two Cities" knitter
63 Bound
65 Business opening
66 Merrill in "Butterfield 8"
68 Affect
69 Dogged CPA?
72 Commercial lip-syncing?
75 90 Across, e.g.
76 Bare
78 Porthos and Athos, e.g.
79 Name of two of Henry's wives
80 Sweet girl of song
83 Rather
84 Rhinoplasty subjects
86 Pomade kin
87 ___ room
88 Oklahoma tribe
90 Midge

92 Freestyle-skier Bergoust
94 Balaam's rebuker
95 Dickens place needs a new roof?
97 Corrective button
101 Put on
102 Sound science
103 Star-studded
105 Marzipan flavor
108 Caesar's existence
109 Bridge
110 Palindromic preposition
111 Novelist O'Flaherty
112 It's near the tee
114 Of birth
116 Highly rated ones
117 Chat-room buddies?
120 Casting needs for "Cocoon"?
123 Dancer, for one
124 Spenser's "The ___ Queen"
125 Parsley-family member
126 Renegades
127 Travel authority
128 Jalopy dings

DOWN

1 Certain Wall Streeters
2 "Modern Maturity" reader
3 At any rate
4 Stuff
5 Simple add-on
6 Isn't selfish
7 Fortune-teller's card
8 "Oh, dear"
9 Collapses
10 What begins in juin
11 ___ Plaines
12 Cozy
13 Low-calorie
14 Neighbor of Minn.

15 Kind of neckline
16 Airfield areas
17 ___ English
18 Harden
19 Michaelmas daisy
24 Larenz in "The Postman"
28 Italian car, familiarly
31 Blackthorne fruits
33 Made
34 Independent nation since 1991
35 "Hey ___" (1954 song)
36 Put away
38 Env. abbr.
39 Intended
40 Mme., in Monterrey
44 Tease
45 Shakespeare's "sweet sorrow"
46 20th-century French battle site
47 "Casey at the Bat" autobiographer
49 Taj Mahal builder Jahan

50 Request at a fast-food outlet
53 Ivan's country home
54 Where Helen Keller grew up
55 Lives
56 Snaps
58 Calla lily, for one
60 Between largos and allegros
62 Corpulent
64 Comes off
67 Lead, to some
70 Prefix with annual
71 Fire spouters
73 Seine feeder
74 ___ -friendly
77 Languors
81 Very much
82 Airport info
85 Femme fatale
89 Gives the nod to
91 Mounted
93 Cartoonist's transparency
95 Chaney of horror films

96 Does a farm task
98 Rest easy?
99 Far from frivolous
100 Clairol-girl features
101 Anno ___
103 Hits the keyboard bar
104 Lie
105 Vigilant
106 Army careerist
107 "West Side Story" song
109 Word with case or well
112 Linda of "Jekyll & Hyde"
113 Lat. and Lith., once
115 Sixties do
116 Newcastle-upon-___
118 NYC summer time
119 ___-Darwinism
120 Not working
121 Taoism founder ___-tse
122 Bit

32 OPPOSITE ENDS   by Michael Collins
Look for seven thematic entries within this amusing polar circle.

ACROSS

1 Parker in "Old Yeller"
5 Teetotaler's order
9 Act like a snake
15 Simoleon
19 K-6: Abbr.
20 Qom home
21 College major, for short
22 Succotash morsel
23 Capitol feature
24 Aussie pastry?
27 Duller of the senses
29 Mound flub
30 Hi-___ graphics
31 Spouted vessels
32 Printers' proofs
33 Drew in
35 Masked man
36 Sheet-music abbr.
37 ___-TASS
39 Stephen in "The Musketeer"
40 Philosopher Rand
41 "___ to Rio": Peter Allen
42 Makes eyes at
44 Ginger Grant, to the islanders?
48 Mutt's moniker
50 Prefix for chutist
52 Maintained the veracity of
53 Start of a Keats title
55 Salon offerings
58 Curt Schilling stat
59 Leave helpless with laughter
63 Officiated
65 Up's partner
67 Fit
70 Ref. set
71 Last number of a barn dance?
75 "___ Lazy River"
76 Legendary
78 "Guys and Dolls" number
79 "Little Big Man" author
81 Trident feature
82 "Am ___ believe . . ."
85 Shade of gray
87 "George M." subject
88 Tapioca source
92 More than fair?
94 Letter opener
95 Roadside area's expenditures?
100 Portable chair
102 Tolkien creature
103 Reliever's place
104 Easter lead-in
105 Big Mack
106 Part of a 105 Across
109 Las ___, NM
111 Certain sax player
114 Tips, e.g.
116 Apache part
117 Thruway warning
118 Keister
119 Tempest site?
120 Aussie weather condition?
124 Coffeehouse performer
125 Road's end?
126 Frosh topper
127 "Zip-___-Doo-Dah"
128 Mayfair metro
129 Hospital supply
130 Smoker in church
131 Can't do without
132 First grader's reward

DOWN

1 Indiana Jones hat
2 Runaway bride
3 Weekend warrior's alert status?
4 Sling mud at
5 Duck
6 Columbian gold
7 She was Mindy
8 2001 Peace Nobelist
9 Kleenex
10 Pol. affiliation
11 Cordwood measure
12 Bit of evidence
13 "Concretions" sculptures
14 As well
15 Red Skelton subject
16 Occupied
17 Explorer Vespucci
18 "The Malcontent" playwright
25 UHF part
26 Charlie Brown, for one?
28 Work like a slave
34 Half a hard rain?
35 Memory unit
38 ". . . and make it snappy!"
40 Chicken
43 Screw-up
44 ___ loading (marathoner's prep)
45 Loan word
46 On behalf of
47 ___ Hashanah
48 Shade of green
49 ___-Kit (police face-maker)
51 Leaf through
54 RC Cola soda
56 Tends to the fairway
57 "Cock-a-doodle-doo!" time
60 Ver-r-r-y interesting excuse?
61 Pop up
62 Has a hankering
64 Anonymous one
66 Piping sound
68 Well-used pencil
69 Blueprint detail, for short
72 Prolific patentee
73 Entomological stage
74 Galba's predecessor
77 Angular lead-in
80 Diva Ponselle
83 "42nd Street" dance
84 Ab ___ (from the top)
86 Shake off
89 Kansas motto word
90 Jeanne d'Arc and others: Abbr.
91 Polly, to Tom
93 Resigned
95 Take another trip over
96 Coming or going
97 Talk like Porky
98 How some things are made
99 "Good ___!"
101 Enjoy a feast
105 Took bold steps
107 It has a psuedopod
108 Not so bad
110 Snake that may be a king
111 Road to Fairbanks
112 Eerie-sounding bird
113 Clear wrap
115 Hook and Cook: Abbr.
117 ___-Ball (arcade game)
121 "Newsworld" network
122 Toss the bull
123 Bridal bio word

33 "YOU'VE GOT MAIL!"   by Norman Wizer

These e-mail letters have something in common with a certain luncheon meat.

ACROSS

1 Pig house material
6 Of birth
11 Dirty bed?
15 Lester Young of bop
19 Outline
20 It may be airtight
21 Megalopolis
22 Portnoy's creator
23 **E-mail heading #1: Part 1**
27 Chemical in car paint
28 Floyd of basketball
29 Devours
30 Summer house?
33 Acord in "The Arizona Kid"
34 Multi-purpose vehicle
35 **Heading #1: Part 2**
46 Pickling solution
47 Road's end?
48 Record speed
49 One of AA's 12
51 Expenditures
52 Rejection notices
55 One, in Cologne
57 New Rochelle campus
58 **E-mail heading #2: Part 1**
63 "A Summer Place" star
64 Lead-in for form
65 State-of-the-art
66 Biggest loser, in Hearts
67 Plays
70 Notwithstanding
73 Request
77 Hopalong's pal
79 Jack or jenny
80 Madrid loc.
83 **Heading #2: Part 2**
90 Colonist Hutchinson
91 Coal scuttle
92 Vituperate
93 Lucine of opera
94 "Get your red-___!"
95 Shamus
97 Andersson in "Persona"
99 Computer nuts
100 **E-mail heading #3: Part 1**
106 "The Blue Max" setting
107 Hawaiian frigate bird
108 Noon, on the Appian Way
109 Pinches
112 Shows off muscles
115 Mentored
121 **Heading #3: Part 2**
125 Shower
126 Finger
127 "I've got my ___ you!"
128 Rind remover
129 Breslau river
130 Kind of friendly?
131 Onsets
132 Clipped

DOWN

1 Charon's river
2 Donahue of "Hawaiian Eye"
3 Julia of "Tango Bar"
4 Ben-Gay target
5 Get off one's chest?
6 Scots negative
7 Ecclesiastic robe
8 White formal attire
9 First lady's son
10 One-dimensional
11 Victorian staff
12 Like crankcases
13 Follower of Aaron
14 Aristotle's school
15 Air
16 Furlong's forty
17 Caesar's final jeopardy question?
18 "Little ___ of Horrors" (1986)
24 Savanna relative
25 Withered
26 "Mon Oncle" star
31 Aurora, to Ajax
32 Win, à la Ian Thorpe
35 "Baby Take ___" (Temple film)
36 Straightened out
37 Book page
38 Former Penn State coach
39 Modernists
40 "He doth ___ on none": Shak.
41 Texas river
42 Spume
43 Throw off
44 "___ Like Alice" (1950)
45 Roberts of "Fawlty Towers"
50 Young salmon
53 Jeu de mots
54 2002 skeleton gold medalist
56 Absolutely not
59 "Yippee!"
60 Munson in "Gone With the Wind"
61 Athena's pet
62 Sloshed
67 Coworker of Happy
68 Hal Foster prince
69 Cong. term
71 Homburg holder
72 Upper-left key
73 New Delhi nanny
74 "___ methinks, I feel a little ease.": Shak.
75 Chess grandmaster Abhijit
76 Like most home aquariums
78 French nobleman
80 LCM chair designer
81 Dallas NHL team
82 Hidden
84 Drum-in method
85 Conceit
86 Roy and Reiner
87 Came down to earth
88 Kharagpur queen
89 RSVP enclosure
96 "The Shining" is one
98 Here, in Dijon
101 Leather piercers
102 The Preserver, in Hinduism
103 Was in arrears
104 Hacked it?
105 Manipulate checks
109 Caen's neighbor
110 Jazz trumpeter Jones
111 Hangover?
112 ___ Blanc wine
113 "Fallen Embers" singer
114 Slumgullion
116 Fanged ophidians
117 Great Salt Lake state
118 Pita sandwich
119 Potato hiller
120 Gyrate
122 West. alliance
123 Ten thousand chiliads
124 Clinic employees

ACROSS

1 Flirty gesture
5 Refuse in the cornfield
9 Must
14 Monastery's main man
19 "On the Waterfront" director Kazan
20 Per
21 "Rich Man, Poor Man" novelist Shaw
22 Wrinkly fruit
23 Cheerful charioteer?
25 Kelly in "High Society"
26 Pauline's problem
27 Tolerate Buchanan?
28 Word of gratitude at Starbucks?
30 "The Simpsons" outburst
31 "Calm down!"
32 Baited a state trooper
33 Ambusher in the bushes
37 Showed
38 Barbra's "Funny Lady" costar
40 Popeye's tooter
44 Buttery Jimmy Webb song?
47 Not so loco
48 Pizzeria fixtures
49 Cyberspace address
50 Lancelot and Elton John
51 Fax originator
52 Beginning of life?
53 Sticks around
55 Poughkeepsie school
57 Woolly mammal
58 Antonio in "Evita"
60 Marisa of "My Cousin Vinny"
62 Made a pointed response
64 Enough foie gras for everyone?
69 Sissy's "Coal Miner's Daughter" role
70 Seuss title creature
71 Bro., for one
72 Tram filler
73 "Bus Stop" star
76 Poker pennies
78 1847 Melville novel
82 Less fresh
84 Distinctive atmosphere
86 Its job is taxing
87 "___ Fashioned Love Song"
88 One way to avoid tipping
89 Top-flight fight?
92 Looks both ways?
93 Layers of ovoids
94 "The Laughing Cavalier" painter
95 "Fire and Rain" singer
96 Sticky-tongued critter
98 Café Americain visitor
99 Unc's kid
100 French painter's soliloquy?
105 Flaunt monikers
110 "___ we a pair?"
111 Charged
112 Northerners
113 Big bill
114 Lowdown joint?
115 Larger-than-life
116 Aretha Franklin's sister
117 Huston's "Prizzi's ___"
118 Christmas stamps
119 Scout's recitation
120 Track event

DOWN

1 Fly traps
2 "Why should ___ you?"
3 Foch of "Spartacus"
4 Madeline of "Blazing Saddles"
5 Geo shelter
6 First name in talk
7 Gravy server
8 Northern ___
9 The briny
10 Deck out
11 Type of song or dive
12 Clock click
13 Two-cents worth
14 8 Down is one
15 Place for dough to grow
16 Hal's "Walk On By" partner
17 "Don't bet ___!"
18 Prefix with photo
24 Dairy handfulls
28 Pack down
29 Big mo. for 86 Across
31 Near the beginning
33 Air problem
34 Basilica area
35 Father of "gangsta" rap
36 Dash
37 Vicar's assistant
38 Gumbo pod
39 Kind of hysteria
41 Owing
42 Squirt
43 Dropped the ball
45 Pizza ___
46 Nice Buick?
47 Cape in Colombia
51 Woodland deities
53 Combat zone
54 Folks in photos, usually
56 Outdated atlas abbr.
59 Offers?
61 2002 Grammy winner
63 "Horsefeathers!"
64 Trunks inside the trunk
65 Invent
66 Neb. neighbor
67 Wafer type
68 Bit players
69 Comes up short
74 Drop from the sky
75 Cather's "One of ___"
77 Winding curve
79 Mobster's main squeeze
80 Pancake topper
81 Baltic Sea feeder
83 Heed
85 People with itchy feet?
87 Blown away
89 Felt around the head?
90 Dice throw
91 Tolerate
93 Monopoly token
97 Riverbank romper
98 Counting everything
99 "Shut up!"
100 Sonic speed
101 Florence's river
102 It's a gas on Broadway
103 Gnu hair
104 "Diana" singer
105 Auto parts brand
106 Carpe ___
107 Internally pink
108 Treater's words
109 High sch. exam
112 Corp. honcho

35 AND THE WINNER IS . . .   by Fran and Lou Sabin
An award-winning mix of humor, originality, and challenge.

ACROSS

1 In-box items
6 Beach bucket
10 Criticism
14 Negotiations
19 Two cents
20 Dealing with
21 Oasis visitor, perhaps
22 Fond farewell
23 Boxer's highest honor?
25 Scout's honor
27 "That's all she ___!"
28 De Brunhoff classic
30 Short bounce
31 Freedom seeker
34 Vote total
35 Poseidon, to Zeus
39 Andean abodes
40 Hat-trick number
41 "The Social Contract" author
42 Four-legged races
43 Freestyle-skiing maneuver
45 Nihil ending
46 Storklike bird
47 Punkie
48 Ultimate
49 Trattoria sauce
51 Give two thumbs down
52 Sign of good taste?
56 Erstwhile
57 Cattle prod
58 Hautbois
59 Discordia, to Greeks
60 "___ & Sense" magazine
61 Zaire river
63 Fifth-century vandal
64 NBA star Iverson
65 Entertained
67 Romain de Tirtoff
68 Rose Murphy's love
69 "Time!" signal
72 Rabbit's foot, e.g.
73 Navy award?
75 Palindromic play title
76 Cause for a citation
77 The Altar
78 Alpine passes
79 Walt Kelly's philosopher
80 Niki de Saint-Phalle painting
81 Yellow diamond award
85 Like Batman and Robin
86 Systematic
90 "A Night at the Opera" tune
91 Author du Maurier
92 Rain makers
93 Imps
94 Siberian sledder
95 Tpk. infraction
96 Calendar since 1000 B.C.
97 Hummer's instrument
98 Peace offering?
102 Tannenbaum topper
107 Sheepish
108 Wrapped up
109 Robert ___
110 "Griffith Gaunt" author
111 Beau Brummell
112 Raises
113 Airline info, slangily
114 Until now

DOWN

1 1997 W. Smith film
2 Buffalo-Syracuse dir.
3 U.K. solons
4 Shows greater patience
5 Lines of descent
6 Faux gems
7 Laver rival
8 Midori on ice
9 Of humble birth
10 Gaylord Ravenal, e.g.
11 Segments
12 "M*A*S*H" actor
13 Dillinger's nemesis
14 Off-limits listings
15 Modifies
16 Bowler or boater
17 "Animal House" barrel
18 Woo
24 Demurrals
26 Drive-___ window
29 Le Carré's Leamas
31 Out to lunch
32 Montenegro neighbor
33 Award for a soldat
34 Snap
35 "You're joking!"
36 "Jinx" award
37 Island aka Rapa Nui
38 Stock price movers
40 Baseball deal
41 Letter train
43 Foray
44 "Great Seal" bills
47 Tallboy
49 Hayfever cause
50 Dashiell's contemporary
52 Lost enthusiasm
53 India's first P.M.
54 Caesar's last word
55 Record sleeve
56 Manuscript sheets
60 Play with water
62 Hayride bundle
65 Jamaican sectarians
66 Microsoft, e.g.
67 Ben-Gurion carrier
68 Superior to
70 City on the Willamette
71 Weather-worn
73 Actor Crawford, to friends
74 Windows XP symbols
77 Has another birthday
79 Crow young
82 Dragonflies
83 Bag brand
84 Water lilies
85 Secret society of Naples
87 It leads to a sum
88 Anthony of "Oliver Twist"
89 Hold
91 Bedazzle
93 "The Pearl Fishers" composer
94 Put aside
96 Busy joint
97 "The Mocker Mocked" painter
98 Approval
99 Roe
100 Coal container
101 Sack
103 Nature
104 Scotland's longest river
105 "The Sultan of Sulu" playwright
106 Part of AARP

36 REAGANOMICS   by Gayle Dean
A memorable similitude from the Great Communicator.

ACROSS

1 Took an easy gait
6 Castle guard
10 Tall tale
14 Convention
19 Papas in "Anne of the Thousand Days"
20 Songstress Fitzgerald
21 Calculator key
22 Umbilicus
23 Simpleton
24 True and actual
25 Pick a PEAR?
26 Metallic sound
27 **Start of a Ronald Reagan quote**
31 Additionally
32 Vole relative
33 Stitch
34 Put the cuffs on
35 Beatles hit
37 Opportune
40 Oklahoma city
41 Cetacean social visit?
44 **Quote continued**
47 Banana oil, for one
49 Fatima's husband
50 Sheep shelters
51 Writing on the wall
52 Canasta card
53 Screen
54 First Lady's garden?
55 Nurses a drink
56 Misty
57 Withers
58 Homer, to Bart
59 Green Gables' girl
60 Luau dance
61 Get one's bearings
62 **Quote continued**
66 Imperfection
69 Move fall's fall
70 Easter bloomer
71 Blubber
74 Walt Disney's middle name
75 Ill-mannered kids
77 Long car, for short
78 Where Enceladus lies
79 Thistledown
80 Archibald ___ (Cary Grant)
81 Fundy attraction

82 Word in a Grace Metalious title
83 Capt. Kirk kept one
84 Scallop feature
85 **Quote continued**
87 Potent ending
88 Yosarian's friend
89 Flat-bottom boats
91 Type of thermometer
92 Not wholesale
95 Insect's secretion
96 Giant who wore "4"
97 Samuel's teacher
100 **End of quote**
105 Quality
106 Kiri Te Kanawa, e.g.
107 Gabfest
108 Get on a soapbox
109 Lessing's Mellings
110 Holiday times
111 Adore
112 Gunpowder ingredient
113 Lightning streaks
114 Nutcracker suite
115 Artichoke buds
116 Paid out

DOWN

1 Boundary
2 University of Maine locale
3 Like a sheet of stamps
4 Tautomer
5 Roman silver coin
6 Brownie point
7 It's found in bars
8 Rickman or Ruck
9 Magic charm
10 Spread out
11 Drinks in the LEAS?

12 Tropical fruit
13 Suctioned off
14 Foggy
15 Ella Phant's friend
16 Unorthodox
17 Dude
18 A very lodge animal?
28 Bite
29 Looks both ways?
30 Command
36 "Right on!"
37 Fermented soybean cake
38 Kindles wrath
39 Beefeater
42 Roswell visitor?
43 Center
44 Scored 100 or 1
45 Faro card
46 Auctioneer's word
48 Compete in moguls
52 Strindberg's "Miss ___"
53 Put on weight
55 In a ___ (dour)

56 Bodybuilders
57 Become threadbare
59 Bows
60 Huckleberry's family
61 Frogner Park locale
62 Deed
63 Used a rotoscope
64 Flies without propulsion
65 Drew a bead on
66 Canada's highest falls
67 Old Possum
68 Where to find a lunula
71 Cupid, to Vixen
72 "___ bitten, twice shy"
73 Jethro of "The Beverly Hillbillies"
75 Like R. L. Stevenson, as a child
76 Roofing slate

77 Margarita ingredient
78 Island in the Tyrrhenian
80 Turkish coins
81 Three-wheeler
82 Helpings
84 Does a tire job
85 Syr Darya's outflow
86 "Portnoy's Complaint" author
90 First-born
93 Authoritative proclamation
94 Buzz off
96 "Bellefleur" author
98 Grow dark
99 Sluggish
100 Original Woodstock performer
101 Iowa city
102 Tar's greeting
103 Pinch pennies
104 Drop acid
105 Soda can feature

37 TIC-TAC-TOE   by Jim Page
If you need help with 30 Across ask Josh Hartnett.

ACROSS

1 Remote
4 ___ deal (signs)
9 Casa chamber
13 Storylines
18 Nabokov novel
19 Old pro
20 Bolt holder
21 Blakley in "Nashville"
22 X
25 In full view
26 Louvre Pyramid designer
27 Baseball's "Little Giant"
28 ___ Major
29 Breastbones
30 O
33 Hamilton's last affair
34 CIA precursor
35 "Lord, ___?" Matt. 26:22
36 Shackled
41 Sterile states
43 Office part-timer
44 Floor square
45 Bite on
49 Bellybutton
51 Clichéd
52 Paul of "Melvin and Howard"
53 Upper-deck section
56 Complained
59 Three-sharps key: Abbr.
60 Spanish surrealist
61 Prefix for lateral
63 ___ de France
64 Pebbles' pet
65 O
68 German philosopher
72 Part of APR
74 Menu phrase
75 Scams
76 "I am a villain; yet ___": Shak.
77 Whitethroat and yellowthroat
81 Manning of football
83 Daisylike flower
84 Eurasian range
85 "No such luck!"
87 Choir song
88 Mens sana in corpore ___

89 Don Corleone
91 Pea soup ingredient
96 Washboard muscle
98 Cuomo or Puzo
99 Merloni of baseball
102 Work station
103 X
108 Nissan model
111 Emerald ___, NC
112 PC key
113 "___ Easy": Ronstadt
114 Daisy type
115 X
118 Clothes piles
119 Creamy cheese
120 Able to handle (a job)
121 Saxophonist Macero
122 "Maids a-milking" group
123 Electronics giant
124 ". . . lifts to the light ___-bred face": Whitman
125 EMT destinations

DOWN

1 Cyclist Casartelli
2 Milton's "___ Eve"
3 Kramden and Waite
4 Morticia's cousin
5 Crummy, in RR slang
6 Journey to Vanity Fair?
7 Hockey teams, e.g.
8 Parabola
9 It drops a bundle?
10 Cordial flavor
11 Brasi in "The Godfather"
12 Had a Reuben
13 For now
14 X
15 Something else

16 Arctic bird
17 Bee bristle
19 Tarnish
23 Sediment
24 Zhou En-lai's successor
29 Pump type
31 "___ for Lawless": Grafton
32 Appearances
33 Brood mare
37 Swear by
38 "Big Fat ___" (2002)
39 "Legally Blonde" heroine
40 Quitclaim
41 Appropriate
42 Seaside swamp
45 Wearing
46 Sphere starter
47 Mideast land
48 O
50 ___ Cruz
51 Dallas sch.
53 Repairman

54 Whale
55 Cuba libre ingredient
57 Right a wrong
58 City in Belgium
60 Allocate
62 Sumac symptom
66 Russian range
67 Introductory course
69 Utah ski spot
70 Violinist Gow
71 Semester
73 Green and Brown
77 Newman-Woodward film
78 Suk shopper
79 "The Fountainhead" author
80 Rama's wife
82 Rio Grande tributary
83 Ramamorph
86 Sheep's clothing?
89 Card to swipe

90 Octopus ejection
92 Restored
93 Curt
94 Brass lubricators
95 "Do ___ Disturb"
97 Scant
99 Mississippi statesman
100 At-the-scene
101 Irish province or coat
104 Cleveland secretary of state
105 Speed Wagon
106 ___-Japanese War
107 Screwballs
108 Arty Manhattan district
109 CEO center
110 Trig
111 Netsuke box
115 ___ Warburg
116 Gilberto Mendoza's org.
117 Sprint rival

38 COURT CASES by James Connolly
If you think a service break is only R&R, you may have trouble with this one.

ACROSS

1 Mr. Ed's friend
7 Regarding
11 Potato-peeling GIs
14 Pelvic prefix
19 Entrance to Hades
20 Bad news for ball teams
22 It'll knock you out
23 Prepare for publication
24 Michael-Marin comedy team?
26 Play hooky
28 ___ serif
29 Whittles down
30 Neighbor of 69 Down
33 NL monogram
34 Baloney
35 Singer DiFranco
36 Ivan signs a rental agreement?
41 Serenade the moon
44 Every señorita has one
46 Age or food follower
47 "May ___": Enya
48 Justice Black
49 Made a putt
50 Pressure unit
51 New England catch
52 Key opening?
53 Handkerchief ltr.
54 Boris covers some split ends?
56 Blockhead
57 Tikkanen of the NHL
58 Castel Gandolfo resident
59 Canal mule
60 Honors formally
62 Bamako's country
64 Speak without fluency
68 High-pH substance
69 Troubadour's verse
72 Project conclusion?
73 Heed the hypnotist
75 Piercing site
78 "Tiny Alice" playwright
79 Monica shy of the mark?
83 Prefix meaning "large"
84 Roswell sightings
85 Doves and hawks
86 Corona quantity
87 Exhume
88 Tabloid fodder
89 Lecher's look
90 Main line
91 Mozart interpreter Claudio
92 Having one sharp
93 Arthur gets off to a fast start?
96 Santa ___ winds
97 Fontanne's partner
98 Contempo-rary art?
99 Miami Sound Machine leader
101 Half a Beatles "White Album" title
104 Bring into the world
106 Soundboard controls
108 Jimmy on the fence?
111 Feudal tenant
115 Concave navel
116 See 29 Across
117 Channel crosser of 1926
118 Minuscule
119 Old NOW cause
120 ___ majesty (high crime)
121 Diva Scotto

DOWN

1 Mars' bailiwick
2 "___ been robbed!"
3 Called the shots
4 Sonia in "Gabriela"
5 Like a mainspring in a stopped watch
6 Go in turns
7 With the bow
8 "Hungry I Reunion" comic
9 Item on a rack
10 Ballroom dance
11 Commissioner Ueberroth's predecessor
12 Bake-sale orgs.
13 W-2 info
14 Under wraps
15 Colleague of Aramis
16 It may be hanging or dimpled
17 Artist Magritte
18 NOW and WHO, for two
21 Sunshine State city
25 Removed some frosting
27 Dressy shoe
30 Dr. Olsen of NASA
31 SAG, for one
32 Venus and Björn adopt a Colonial style?
33 Rundown neighborhood, informally
34 Herculean tasks
37 Goes on and on and on
38 Tribal tales
39 Hammer partner
40 Raison d'___
41 Rumor about Steffi?
42 ". . . lost at ___ of tick-tack": Shak.
43 Fluctuates wildly
45 NYPD rank
48 Start of an incantation
51 "Amscray!"
54 Mutton cut
55 Adlai's '56 running mate
56 Do in
58 Ballet bend
61 Act as lookout
63 Alamogordo event
65 Leather ruiner
66 Bass and Harp
67 Crow bars
69 Jidda native
70 Like Keebler's tree folk
71 ___ for sore eyes
74 Like fish sticks
76 Galápagos creature
77 Port Moresby resident
80 Colleague of Agatha
81 Tea complement
82 Critter with a scut
83 Space station in the ocean
85 Sarajevo locale
87 Play the market, in a way
90 Gland atop the kidney
93 Meadows who was Alice
94 Pulls down
95 Letter signoff
97 Pig language?
100 City on the Ruhr
101 "Sit ___!": Fonzie
102 "Stand By Me" singer King
103 Nice moon
104 Duel memento
105 Least bit
106 Brothers
107 "___ sow, so shall . . ."
109 "Crooklyn" director
110 Have chits out
112 Mexicali Mrs.
113 Space-bar neighbor
114 Pastoral setting

39 OF HUMAN BONDAGE by Ernest Lampert

71 Across received the Best Female Stand-Up award in 1990.

ACROSS

1 Potemkin Mutiny site
7 Put one past?
11 Animal track
16 Id moderator
19 Contradicts
20 It goes with the wind
21 City on the Ganges
22 Ivanov of ballet
23 **Start of a quote**
26 90° from SSE
27 A's neighbor
28 Zinger
29 Aeschines, e.g.
30 Novello in "Once a Lady"
31 "Like ___ love it!"
32 Like fall-foliage tours
35 **More of quip**
37 Cowan Award org.
38 Okinawa capital
40 Seine tributary
41 **More of quote**
47 Register
51 Mustard genus
52 Stuck one's neck out
55 Skewbald
56 Curtain time
57 Merida
59 A great dist.
61 Tiger of Cooperstown
62 Dreadlocked cultist
64 Remove a typo
65 Martian
67 Crusher of "Star Trek: TNG"
68 **More of quote**
71 **Auth. of quote**
73 Snaps
76 Special interest groups
77 Takes the lion's share
78 Hamelin river
82 "Enquirer" couple
84 Esau's wife
85 Opts
88 Pheasant brood
89 Lesson
91 Footless
93 Jocks
95 Alias
97 **More of quote**
99 Strong as ___
101 Modem measure
102 Extra qtrs.
103 **More of quote**
108 Simonize
111 35mm camera
114 Aleutian island
115 Leachman in "High Anxiety"
117 Outkast music
118 First name in "Pleasure"
120 Multipurpose truck
121 **End of quote**
124 Cross ___
125 "Froggy ___ courtin'. . ."
126 Faulkner's "Requiem for ___"
127 Doubles' double trouble?
128 Rather than
129 Persuasion
130 Portrayal
131 Feature of Polyphemus

DOWN

1 Small antelope
2 China city
3 "Don Carlos" princess
4 Capital of Fiji
5 Western hats
6 Obs. fireproofing
7 Arrival at Orly
8 Baja bar
9 Chang's twin
10 Sales model
11 Sardine
12 Head lines
13 Useless
14 Taxing
15 "Ultra cool!"
16 Académie student
17 Italian Riviera city
18 Undisguised
24 Scots uncle
25 Richards in "Jurassic Park"
30 Halcyon
33 Muslim judges
34 Jeer
36 Valise
37 Calls on
39 Mezzo Marilyn
41 Lift at Deer Valley
42 "Portrait of ___ Bates": Wyeth
43 Some are saturated
44 Horned Frogs' college
45 Kind of race
46 Blow up
48 No sound-alike
49 "Wouldn't ___ Nice?": Beach Boys
50 His ___ (cribbage jack)
53 Like Siena, originally
54 Not natural, in a way
58 Darjeeling store
60 Headed up
63 Precinct alert
66 Neoteric
69 High note
70 Score ending
71 Furls
72 Starts in again
73 Arizona Indian
74 Lay ___ thick
75 Dry prefix
77 "I ___ Symphony": Supremes
79 Rama's wife
80 Course at St. Andrews
81 Flake out
83 Procrastinator's word
86 Old comm. device
87 Scares off
90 Swann of football
92 Scree
94 Helsinki cathedral
96 Camel sponge
98 Smelly
100 Aviaton fuel ingredient
103 Hose hue
104 Paravane
105 Sunflower seed
106 Métier
107 Knoll nymph
109 Hall-of-Fame Lion QB
110 NYSE first-timer
111 Underground gate
112 "Waiting for ___": Odets
113 "Touched by an Angel" star
116 Chrysler's logo
119 Scads
121 Meteor. station
122 Cousin of the tuna
123 Bogey

FOR DUMMIES . . .   by Raymond Hamel
"Author! Author!"

ACROSS

1 Blues great Taj
6 Tiff
10 Béla Fleck's instrument
15 Crones
19 Anne Klein style
20 "Harper's Bazaar" rival
21 More glacial
22 Somewhat
23 "Carpeting for Dummies" author?
25 Ticket: Sl.
26 Chess act
27 Put out a batter
28 "La ___ Bonita": Madonna
30 Five make fifty
31 "The Ghost and Mrs. ___" (1947)
32 Shreds and tatters
34 "Do Cats Have ___?": Dixon
35 "___ nuit"
36 Treed
39 Dominant
40 Like city driving
42 Density symbols
43 Novelist Kobo
44 Stilo or Punto
46 Toward the mouth
47 Cerebral layers
49 NBC overseer
50 Lowbrow
54 "Manners for Dummies" author?
56 Prairie tribe
58 Love feast
59 Car-seat user
60 Make higher in one's estimation
63 Drooped
64 Car with a meter
67 "Fashion for Dummies" author?
70 Bobby ___
71 Sirens
73 Free from worry
74 Bozo
76 In need of a diet
77 Gong shape
78 "Watercraft for Dummies" author?
84 Grading system
86 ___ ipsa loquitur
89 Prestige
90 Cut in half by a magician, say
91 Carried
92 Nicholas in "Vertical Limit"
93 Melt fish
94 "Le Million" director
98 Rock bottom
100 Microwave ray
101 Microphone inventor Berliner
102 Univera, for one
103 Quick-and-dirty
105 Land's end?
106 Roadie's responsibility
107 Keyboard goof
108 Cough-syrup ingredient
112 He wrote about Sheba
113 Woody vine
115 "Astrology for Dummies" author?
117 Close by
118 World record?
119 Utah ski resort
120 Stephen King's "___ Macabre"
121 Tall birds
122 Owen in "Queen Kelly"
123 Painted Desert formation
124 Union general at Bull Run

DOWN

1 Bryn ___
2 Wings of Love
3 Claymore "basket"
4 Hors d'oeuvre with olives
5 "Tender Moment" singer Parnell
6 Embroider
7 Simplicity
8 Ready to roll
9 Attacks verbally
10 Action at the auction
11 Most critical
12 Least critical
13 "Cloning for Dummies" author?
14 Pluto food
15 "Breakfast for Dummies" author?
16 Runneth over
17 Charitable
18 Mono successor
24 Popular '20s auto
29 Jellied garnish
33 "The Devil" Duke of Normandy
35 Words for a black sheep
36 Place de l'Étoile sight
37 What you used to be
38 "Star Trek" collective
41 Cellist Jacqueline du ___
43 Bywords
45 Way in
48 Aquatic newt
50 Dukas ballet (with "La")
51 Othello's lieutenant
52 Tip-top
53 "The London Spy" author Ward
55 Pitched quarters?
57 After moon or muck
61 Phil or Joe of baseball
62 Narc's org.
63 Cropless fields
64 Desi Arnaz's homeland
65 His dragon was killed by Cadmus
66 "Writing Novels for Dummies" author?
68 Execute perfectly
69 Rent sharers
71 Trim off
72 Fix the facade
75 Card-holding display
77 "Demolition for Dummies" author?
79 Whirlybird perches
80 Radioactive process
81 Burden
82 Retin-A target
83 Streak
85 Hole puncher
87 Blofeld in "Thunderball"
88 White terrier
91 "GoldenEye" star
94 Do a crude oil job?
95 Rapper Marshall Mathers
96 Indian antelope
97 Transfix
99 Radio antenna
100 Vespas
104 "How Dry I Am" syllable
106 "Good grief!"
109 Hit on the head
110 St. John the Divine area
111 Cancún couple
114 Quick-wink connection
116 Car club est. in 1902

41 UNEMPLOYMENT LINES by Fred Piscop

"A worker is a part-time slave." — Bob Black

ACROSS

1 Liquids and gases
7 Old German coin
13 Qty.
16 Phi Beta Kappa concern
19 Michael in "The Lost World"
20 Worked over
21 Silky-haired feline
23 Unemployment line
25 Flexibility
26 Red giant, e.g.
27 Passé platters
28 Grand Dragon's org.
30 Syr. neighbor
31 Fajita wrap
34 In unison
35 Rap session?
39 Unemployment line
42 Some bow ties
46 Don the feed bag
47 Tiny pest
48 Up to
49 Former Houston ice man
50 Comics bark
51 Words to an old chap?
53 Has a bug
54 Unemployment line
61 Juliet Jones' sister
62 Pupil's place
63 Intimate of H. Miller
64 Initials for Nipper
65 Made an old flame new?
67 Hindu ascetic
69 Determine the concentration of
73 Quebec place name abbr.
74 Sheryl Crow's "___ Wanna Do"
75 Stuff to be crunched
76 Kind of grad school
77 Unemployment line
82 Phone, slangily
84 Krait cousins
85 Hollywood's Thurman
86 In ___ (actually)
87 End of some URLs
88 Darjeeling duds
90 Troy, NY campus
91 Plucks out of the air
94 Unemployment line
99 Singing soldier of the '60s
100 Lake in SE Africa
101 Belgian Pyrenees, for one
106 Green around the gills
107 The Baltics, once: Abbr.
108 Vamp's accessory
109 Kirlian photography image
110 Sgt. Preston, for one
114 Unemployment line
118 Up
119 Soprano Tebaldi
120 Software swiper
121 "___ you nuts?"
122 Fair-hiring letters
123 Hurricane, to a beach
124 Has a bite of

DOWN

1 Volunteer senator
2 Slowly, in music
3 Open a gate
4 Like helium
5 Morse tap
6 Baste, perhaps
7 Rock-boring tool
8 Cackleberry producers
9 Modifying wd.
10 Eyeballs
11 As a whole
12 Laid anew, as pipe
13 Computer program, informally
14 Singer Etheridge
15 Cut in thirds
16 Rickey need
17 Lobbying org.
18 "___ takers?"
22 Ice star Hughes
24 "Name Game" singer
29 Profit
32 "___ To Extremes": Joel
33 Warneke of baseball
34 Toward the stern
36 "___ I can help it!"
37 Wound-up sidewinder
38 Some bends
40 Ex-Spice Girl Halliwell
41 Suffix meaning "name"
42 Work like Blondie
43 Time on shore
44 Teed off
45 Fermented fare
50 Not pres.
51 Sidi ___, Morocco
52 The slammer
53 Way out
55 Capone cohort
56 Like a new recruit
57 Helping hand
58 Jack of "double take" fame
59 Verdi aria
60 In base 8
66 "I'll be ___ of a gun!"
67 Dick Fosbury's namesake
68 Needy's need
69 Profs' aides
70 Horsey sect?
71 Knotted up
72 Just beats
74 Hands out
75 "Jurassic Park" letters
77 Celtic priest of yore
78 First senator in space
79 Serving of tea, to a Brit
80 Strike out
81 Sleuth, informally
82 Cuts down
83 Greek playhouses
88 Small collie
89 Delta, but not gamma
90 Brazzi of "Summertime"
91 Roomie, of sorts
92 Suffix with meth- or hex-
93 Monogram of Prufrock's creator
95 Momentary flash
96 City of S India
97 Whopper teller
98 Weather-map line
102 Skating competition
103 Box office buy, slangily
104 Take the stump
105 Blows hard
108 Lessen the force of
110 Wharton School deg.
111 Dinghy thingie
112 Western tribe
113 Swelled head
115 Bummed
116 Fit
117 Madre's hermana

42 PATRIOTS DAYS   by Roger H. Courtney
A genuine tribute to some great Americans.

ACROSS

1 "Star Wars," e.g.
5 "I could ___ unfold": Shak.
10 Stock-car stick-on
15 Gillette brand
19 Excited
20 Old French dance
21 Live to ___ old age
22 Mooneye's cousin
23 Honoree of 43 Down
26 Donned
27 Hold to one's heart
28 Miss World wear
29 Get ___ of
30 "You got that right!"
31 Maverick
32 Divine food
33 Woodstock '69 performer
35 "Old Blood and Guts"
38 Diocese
41 Canvasback's cousin
45 ___ du Diable
46 Telly Savalas role
48 Composer Méhul
49 Russian America capital
52 "Honor Thy Father" author
53 B.A. and Ph.D.
54 "The GI General"
58 PMs
59 Historic London suburb
61 Japanese aborigine
62 Ten-four, for one
64 LL.D. holder
65 Apiece
68 Gain a lap
70 Open-___ shoes
71 Sviglerova of tennis
74 Larry Flynt's magazine
77 Star of "Elephant Boy"
79 Herring type
81 Organist Atkins
83 Most decorated WW2 soldier
87 Coal follower
88 Wal-Mart rival
90 Ziti, for one
91 Sabbatical leave

93 Photographer Adams
94 "Happy Warrior"'s monogram
95 Hiatuses
96 See 43 Down
97 "Unconditional Surrender" general
104 Most hallowed
106 "___ looking at you!"
107 Greek island
112 Generous slice
114 Title for 115 Across
115 Tussaud
116 Trig ratio
117 Pamplona runner
118 University of Penn founder
121 43,560 square feet
122 Return key
123 ___ Aquarius
124 1961 space chimp
125 Robin Williams film
126 Regions: Abbr.
127 Greene of "Bonanza"
128 Devonshire dune

DOWN

1 Wise guys
2 He may be special
3 Chester of "Gunsmoke"
4 Mutually concur
5 "Who Cares?" composer
6 Game of marbles
7 1975 Belmont winner
8 Unprofitable
9 Fuel gas
10 Actor Carvey
11 Work unit
12 Viagara, for one
13 "You've got ___ there"

14 Give for a time
15 Nile River dam
16 University of Virginia founder
17 Like the Nile crocodile
18 Seaport for 99 Down
24 William in "Rain"
25 Cleo's attendant
32 Road Runner box
33 Deli dishes
34 "Times of Your Life" singer
36 Rubik of cube fame
37 Rock rabbit
39 It's right on the map
40 Barely manages
41 Jason's wife
42 Alamogordo event
43 "First in war, first in peace . . ." speaker (with 96-A)
44 ___ majesté
47 Patron saint of Norway

49 Mysore Mr.
50 Arabian sons
51 Platitudes
52 Daly of "Judging Amy"
55 Oohed and ___
56 Like a Christmas tree
57 I
60 Thing, in law
63 ER cases
66 Rat tail?
67 Gulager in "Winning"
69 Strained
72 Empty spots
73 Tête-___
75 The munchies, e.g.
76 "The ___ fruit first falls": Shak.
78 Bandeau
80 Andean land
81 Bologna loc.
82 Weatherbird
84 Facilitate
85 Tree frogs
86 Have a kid

89 Jewish month
92 Takes control
94 Green lights
98 Armed, but not dangerous
99 Omani neighbor
100 Pillow cover
101 Kind of number or killer
102 Yankee, to Pancho Villa
103 Walk-in cooler
105 Hautboys
108 Inquired
109 "The Red House Mystery" author
110 Kremlin dome shape
111 Get the feeling
112 Sports figure?
113 Crazed
115 M&M's parent
116 "Lunch at the Gotham ___": King
119 Gastineau was one
120 Wood of the Stones

43 LAST NAME FIRST   by Jay Sullivan
You can always count on plenty of puns in a Sullivan, Jay puzzle.

ACROSS

1 Order to go
6 Seven-segment crustacean
12 In situ
19 Fuss
21 Bundle up
22 How the New Year is greeted
23 Bette Davis "As You Like It" film?
25 Let go
26 "Five Guys Named ___" (1990 revue)
27 "Mum's the word!"
28 Root word
30 Shopping spots
31 Son of Seth
33 Humorist Bombeck
35 Out
37 Woody Allen "Apollo 13" remake?
44 Mountaineer gear
47 "Tyrant lizard king"
48 Every man (except Adam)
49 Flower cluster
50 Hairy whale film?
54 Section of LA
55 Future butterflies
56 Rite answers
57 Former kiwi kin
58 Disney film?
59 Evening, in Essen
60 One of the Bobbsey twins
61 Big Blue, on the Big Board
62 David Lean epic with dry Champagne music?
66 38 Down and others
68 Jerks
69 Seeks answers
70 Floury big-bucks Eastwood film?
74 "Scrubs" network
75 Square-dance partner
78 "___ Something to Me": Porter
79 WWW whereabouts
80 Salvia species
81 Put in an appearance
82 Sitar and chitarrone
83 Penny portrait
84 Chesty Streisand musical?
87 Former Mogul capital
88 Picture of health
89 Rookie
90 February foursome
91 Film about a Quidditch match?
97 Player's club
98 Latch
99 An officeholder may take it
103 Piano piece
107 Bottom line
108 Sweet talk
109 Courtroom anonym
110 Leading
112 Newman film about a loser lawyer?
118 Citrus hybrid
119 Murky
120 Pooh's pal
121 Make a name for oneself?
122 Took steps
123 Not as old

DOWN

1 Show up
2 Writer's cause for pause
3 Lumberjack tourney
4 Sherlock's shout
5 Fairy queen
6 Panama et al.
7 ___ Na Na
8 Not 'neath
9 Launch site
10 Burden unduly
11 Highest North American peak
12 First Burmese premier
13 Nine-sided figure
14 Surroundings
15 Chicano bears
16 Baroque instrument
17 If not
18 They can get in your hair
20 Follower of Daniel
24 "Driving Miss Daisy" playwright
29 Chewbacca's friend
32 Does a veterinary job
34 "The Practice" roles: Abbr.
35 1958 Pulitzer novelist
36 Some frat men
38 Year in the reign of Nero
39 Animal shelter
40 Goes overboard?
41 Blood classification
42 Saudi neighbor
43 "You don't ___ weatherman . . .": Dylan
44 Poker pronouncement
45 Closing notes
46 Dark, to Donne
51 Containing NH2
52 "___ deal!" ("Don't mention it!")
53 Hoover or Roosevelt
54 Grouse gathering grounds
55 Use a lot
58 Kadiddlehopper
62 Leb' ___ (Franz's farewell)
63 Clean-air agcy.
64 Long-haired male model
65 Opus Award org.
66 Like a llama
67 Cpls.
68 "Truth or ___" (1991)
70 Legally
71 Ready partner
72 Bizarre
73 Gloat
74 Wild org.
75 LAX boarding area
76 On the rampage
77 It's in the eye of the beholder
80 It's on tenterhooks
81 Aria by 106 Down
83 Work of Michelangelo
84 Service song
85 Before, of yore
86 Its point is to make holes
88 The Golden Horde
89 Show off
92 Mull over
93 Sets up
94 Window-dressing
95 Holding the bag
96 Lyric verse
100 Green light
101 Jason Giambi's manager
102 Romance writer Georgette
103 Fill up
104 Compared to
105 Use a shredder
106 "Otello" baritone
111 War party
113 "Catch-22" role
114 Wall St. takeover
115 Lay low
116 Signature piece
117 Good looker

ACROSS

1 Leaves at the altar
6 Kate in "Iris"
13 Raise the cost of
18 1935 Triple Crown horse
19 Fatty
20 Under
22 Intro to a Beethoven symphony?
24 Book cracker
25 Nobelist Sakharov
26 Sphinx-riddle answer
27 Without end
29 "Hey!"
31 Peter of Peter and Gordon
34 Come-___ (inducements)
35 Manuscript encl.
38 Charcoal burner
41 Analogy words
43 Trivial amount
46 Little rascal
47 Plagiarize a Beethoven symphony?
49 In ___ veritas
50 Kind of toast
52 Adherent's suffix
53 LP half
54 Libra neighbor
55 Last Supper query
56 Frat T
58 Monroe, Taylor, and Hayes
60 Paul Harvey's birthplace
63 Instant-replay cameras
66 Piece of cake?
67 ___ kwon do
68 Bouncer's requests
70 Beethoven "Ode to Joy" symphony?
73 Newsy handouts
74 Alumna bio word
75 Pesky kid
76 NYSE counterpart
77 Tickle pink
79 Immunize
82 Ice pick, essentially
84 Blackmore heroine
87 Deck out
88 This and that
91 Addams cousin
93 Schlemiel
94 Turn down
95 Beethoven summer symphony?
98 Man-mouse link
99 Drop the curtain on
100 Phobos orbits it
101 Fairly fast
102 Snooty one
103 Aurora's counterpart
104 Dog-___ (shabby)
106 Osaka Bay port
108 Tilting at windmills
112 "Yoo-___!"
115 Angry with
119 Regally attired
120 Beethoven city symphony?
124 Congress-woman Hooley
125 Refuse
126 Paris divider
127 It's on the Aire
128 Tear, poetically
129 ___-Martin

DOWN

1 Castanet dance
2 "___ a roll!"
3 Friday's org.
4 Swimmer nicknamed "Flipper"
5 Repositories
6 Nursery sound
7 As above
8 Chris craft?
9 Iron pumped by Popeye?
10 Ban-___ (shirt material)
11 Best guess: Abbr.
12 Titter
13 Promise to wed
14 "Search me"
15 Rugrats' pops
16 Regulated co.
17 Do KP work
20 Wind dir.
21 See 17 Down
23 Actress Campbell-Martin
28 Win-place-show bet
30 Polynesian figurine
32 "___ a Woman": Beatles
33 Avery Fisher's field
35 Reagan Library valley
36 Spy Aldrich
37 Beethoven symphony in two parts?
39 Numero uno
40 Come by
42 Class of verbs
43 Beethoven symphony about Adam?
44 Ready to roll
45 Prods into action
47 Death spiral
48 Journalist Tarbell
49 Word on either side of "-à-"
51 A/C measure
54 In a youthful manner
57 Ashe Stadium inits.
59 React to a haymaker
61 A Lennon
62 Joystick wielder
64 i=v/r formulator
65 Stadium near Ashe
68 Blitz, say
69 Inject Novocain
71 Bubbles over
72 Divorcée
78 To a fault
80 Call out
81 Chariot attachment?
83 Naval off.
85 Rex's sleuth
86 Dhow crewman
89 Milky Way part
90 "Wilde" actress Jennifer
92 Young upstart
95 Laces up
96 Veteran
97 At large
100 Stuck it out?
102 Best of seven, say
103 Extradite
105 Divert
107 ___ nova
108 Proof letters
109 Caspian feeder
110 Hungary's Nagy
111 Ox tail?
113 ___ about (roughly)
114 Grid great Graham
116 Get out
117 Carbon's is 6
118 "In that case . . ."
121 Unit of hope?
122 "Later"
123 Dance in socks

45 PULLING RANK   by Alan Olschwang
And pulling a few legs too!

ACROSS

1 Runs out of gas
6 Tormé specialty
10 Like window dummies
14 Did a cobble job
19 Tolerate
20 Cartoon possum
21 "Oh Me Oh My" singer
22 Place for an élève
23 Hit bottom, on the Nasdaq
24 Part of PAYE
25 Magnanimous offer
26 Fix junior's shoes
27 First-class sleuth?
31 Pother
33 To the point
34 Take the odds
35 Indicate
36 ___ Alamos
37 Sit differently?
38 ___ moderna (trendy)
40 Units of magnetic flux
43 Gem State
45 Sapporo sash
46 Shellbacks
47 Screw bean, for one
50 It flies like an eagle?
54 Coin of ancient Rome
56 Latin being
57 Irritate
58 Fuming
60 Manhattan museum
61 Mongolian desert
62 A ship to remember
63 Slip-up
64 Like Soldier Field
68 Assam, e.g.
70 Camelot knight
71 Organic compounds
72 Utter in monotone
73 Whoopi Goldberg film
75 ". . . liquor is quicker" poet
77 Brownish gray
78 Hardtack
79 Deer head?
80 Starter starter
84 Like Cousteau's world
86 Oak Leaf insurance plan?

89 "___ How They Run": Patterson
90 Valued strings
92 Mother of Zephyrus
93 Black
94 Curling shoe
95 MD and ME
96 He makes the calls
98 Japanese courtesy title
99 Not entirely
102 Explorer Johnson
104 Drive out
106 Yang's pal
107 Barred rulers?
112 "Jerusalem Delivered" poet
113 Met highlight
114 Late-night monologist
115 Helicopter assembly
118 Sign on a door
119 Swerve
120 Carroll's "Baby Doll" director
121 Anton's skating partner
122 "The Cloister and the Hearth" author
123 Relax
124 Sky light
125 Incubus, e.g.

DOWN

1 "Wonderful!"
2 Baltimore Hustlers' org.
3 Kitchen appliances
4 Fulda feeder
5 Insurrection
6 Asparagus units
7 Puts on paint
8 Congenial
9 Alpine skier Sailer
10 Garlic section
11 Crescent-shaped opening
12 Supplicant's request

13 "Heart and Soul" is one
14 Striped marine swimmer
15 "___ Eleven" (2001)
16 Game of chance
17 George who was Mary
18 Steel-plow pioneer
28 Dog's best friend
29 David Stern's org.
30 Hangs out
31 Pool of Tears source
32 Pool of Tears bird et al.
39 Weeks per annum
41 Dudes on a dude ranch
42 Bob Hoskins in "Hook"
44 Work down on the farm
45 Wipe out
46 Pixy
47 Sticker ___

48 Come to pass
49 Flyer fakes
51 Wear away
52 A movement, briefly
53 Maureen O'Sullivan's daughter
55 Formerly, formerly
59 Toledo year
61 Star PX?
62 House heads
63 Intervening, in law
64 Roman emperor (79–81)
65 Puerile
66 Chopin's "Black Key" piece
67 Soap on a ___
69 Rijksmuseum city
74 Actress Lupino
76 Ready follower?
78 Tire lip
79 Youngest U.S. president
80 Omsk loc.
81 Biosphere, e.g.

82 Veranda
83 "Captain Blood" star
85 Strike
87 See 93 Across
88 Condemned
91 Twists of fate
94 Drenched
95 Slump
96 Hullabaloo
97 Maya Angelou poem
99 Make ends meet?
100 Hansen of NPR
101 "Hostess with the Mostes' "
103 Take a long look
105 City near Dayton
108 Wheel hub
109 With code or way
110 They ring in the ring
111 Starlet's quest
116 "Starpeace" singer
117 Competed in an 8K

ACROSS

1 Small groups
6 Late bedtime
11 Crime chief
15 River in Normandy
19 "The Chosen" author
20 Early Eastern mercenary
21 Hi-res set
22 Rx bottle
23 **Start of a quote**
25 Helmet wreath
26 It may be necessary
27 School days
28 Wrinkly tangelo
30 Make less dense
32 Corner key
33 Boone, to his buddies
34 Fat substitute
36 Takes a chance
37 **More of quote**
43 Historic Boston Hill
46 Persona's opposites
47 Weaponry stock
48 "___ Fly with Me"
49 Did a clean and jerk
50 "The African Queen" writer
51 "Deep Space Nine" officer
52 **More of quote**
55 Rafts
56 Nothing more than
57 Short ruler
58 Swing to ___
59 Sp. coins
60 Swerved
61 Dissemble
62 ___ Darya River
63 Options
64 Hammer on a slant
65 Paint resin
68 ___-à-porter
69 Regular practice
71 Clarke in "Frankenstein"
74 Dispatch
75 Majorette, perhaps
76 **Source of quote**
78 Fluff
79 "It's either them ___!"
80 Charming
81 Part of the loop
82 It's famous for its cedars
84 Libertine
85 Reporter Starr
87 **More of quote**
89 Jury panelist
90 "Murder" she wrote
91 "Beau Geste" author
92 Nonprofessional org.
95 Poseurs
98 Bird or escapade
100 Ise worshiper
102 Hibernation site
103 He monkeys around?
105 **End of quote**
107 Wile E. Coyote's supplier
108 Intimate
109 Divert
110 Señor Wences has one
111 "The Swiss Family Robinson" author
112 Easter follower
113 French city of denim fame
114 Basket material

DOWN

1 Lickety-split
2 Colgate class
3 Impassive
4 4-time winning Super Bowl coach
5 Lost control
6 Whopper toppers
7 Williamson in "Excalibur"
8 Cherokee Strip city
9 Steely Dan album
10 Prefix for script
11 Spiny cacti
12 Arpel of cosmetics
13 Bakker's ex-org.
14 Deposed
15 Intimidate
16 Bank of Paris
17 Babe in the woods
18 Jed Clampett's daughter
24 "___ about it"
29 Turn psycho
31 End of a Stein line
35 Metal stamps
36 English channel, informally
37 Well-read
38 Doesn't participate
39 Leon in "Peyton Place"
40 Former Turkish premier
41 Big dipper
42 Harold in "Safety First"
43 Backdoor approach to an A
44 Latitude
45 Shoot-___ (western)
46 Olympic charges
49 Treo screen
50 Sim of Scrooge fame
53 ___ up in lavender
54 Enron's ex-exchange symbol
55 Disabled
56 Pedro's cheer
59 Boxster
60 Exclusive
61 Driver St. James
64 Guitarist Farlow
65 Journalist St. Johns
66 Ponti's partner
67 Puckett of baseball
68 Capital of England
70 Moist finish
71 Jazz flutist Herbie
72 A wink and ___
73 Site of Vulcan's forge
75 Rich roll
76 Needlepoint result?
77 Contender
79 Where a roulette bet may be
80 Vacuum-bottle inventor
83 Recants
84 "The Russia House" author
85 Geoffrey of fashion
86 Leases
88 Balm of ___
89 Readies
91 A question of possession
92 Garlic sauce
93 Cassette front
94 Complete
95 It makes a second
96 Salacious
97 Points
99 "Kubla ___": Coleridge
100 Riffraff
101 Regretful miss of song
104 Louvre Pyramid architect
106 Owner of Abbey Road Studios

"MY CARD . . ." by Jim Page
Jim thought up this theme while watching "What's My Line?"

ACROSS

1 Squalid
6 Eggbeater
12 Skeleton surface
15 "10-4" sayer
19 Marathon marketplace
20 Where Noah landed
21 USMC overseer
22 Architectural border
23 James Hansen, ___ "Providence"
25 Mode lead-in
26 Congo waterway
27 Hears loud and clear
28 Key with arrows
29 Kind of sketch
31 Unsched.
32 Words of praise
33 Math subj.
34 "___ and ye shall receive"
35 Harry Weston, ___ "Empty Nest"
39 Designer Norman (1900–72)
42 Richard Gere film
43 Belted out
44 Flowering
46 Greek epic
47 George W. Bush's deg.
49 Donovan, to Ione Skye
51 MTA stop
52 Billy Martin's number
53 Equal a bet
54 White poplar
56 Final: Abbr.
58 Medicates
60 Heir homophone
61 19th hole
62 Snowboard name
65 Dipsomaniacs
66 Tim Taylor, ___ "Home Improvement"
70 Libel
73 Adonal of basketball
74 Blackball
75 Summer camp asst.
78 "Each minute seems ___": Shak.
79 Jimjams
80 Simian activity
82 ___ fide
83 Abner's father
84 Computer terminal?
86 Small part
89 Hwys.
90 Come up again
91 Prepares to go
93 Knife handle
95 Billboard, to some
97 Call back
98 Al Bundy, ___ "Married . . . With Children"
100 Pod resident
101 "Before I Fall In Love" singer Lee
103 Business card abbr.
104 Expensive eggs
105 Punt-return option
108 "The Mists of Avalon" ntwk.
109 Sonia in "The Rookie"
112 Son of Hassam
113 Lace up
114 Jason Seaver, ___ "Growing Pains"
118 Part of NFC
119 Some gametes
120 Hide homes
121 Like "Everything's Eventual"
122 "Time ___ the essence"
123 Chippendales dancers
124 Shakespearean Guinness role
125 "Been There Done That" rapper

DOWN

1 Dallas NBAer, briefly
2 Antiquing "cheater"
3 Bread-and-butter ___
4 Whole lot
5 Charlie Parker
6 Coffee holder
7 Alcibiades, e.g.
8 Heavenly
9 NYC's "Triangle below Canal"
10 NASA scientist's degree
11 Raytheon's NYSE symbol
12 Lava Hot Springs locale
13 Tom Bradford, ___ "Eight Is Enough"
14 Breakfast cheese
15 Ernest Frye, ___ "Amen"
16 Get off the hook?
17 Giantess who wrestled Thor
18 Scottish dance
24 Writer Babel
29 Hours in a Saturn day
30 West Indies island
33 Loopy
35 Kind of cap or circle
36 Composer Jaques-Dalcroze
37 Kettledrum
38 What J. Jeffords turned
40 Windsor loc.
41 Howard Hughes, for one
42 "___ work if you can . . ."
45 Kettle of fish
48 Deprived
50 Spanish peso
54 Lane in "Maracaibo"
55 Resent
57 Contract getter, usually
59 Decide on
63 Map abbr.
64 Father of Eos
65 Grab a cube
66 Portuguese explorer
67 Radiohead album
68 Turn go-with
69 Humperdinck hero
70 "Drat!"
71 Arab prince
72 J.S. Bach played one
75 Swiss Miss drink
76 Lay to rest
77 Biblical weed
79 Greg Medavoy, ___ "NYPD Blue"
81 Nosecount noses
82 Finger painter, e.g.
85 Short homily
87 Bounce off
88 City in Mali
90 Jet-setted
92 Elroy S. Lobo, ___ "B.J. and the Bear"
94 Be a compositor
96 ___ Buena Island
98 Headmaster's conc.
99 Rose of Sharon
102 Aegir's realm
105 Converging points
106 Foofaraws
107 It's split at CERN
110 Prepare for action
111 Arabian province
114 Needham, MA software co.
115 See 102 Down
116 Mount Carmel loc.
117 Souvenir shirt

48 BEWARE THE MARCH OF IDES! by Charles M. Deber
A most clever challenger from a Canadian cruciverbalist.

ACROSS

1 City on the Jumna
6 Gripe
10 "Aroint thee!"
14 Bridges or Greenfield
18 Hodgepodges
19 Cool kind of bear
20 Part of TLC
21 It's the wheel thing
22 BESS
24 MAN
26 Pad
27 Willing to adapt
28 On the lam
29 Tom Brady stats
30 Links
32 Freud's conscience
35 ALLY
39 Actor Zimbalist
43 "Gotcha!"
44 Set
45 Tarzan's troop
46 Guy Fawkes Day feature
48 Gymnast with a theme
50 7th-century French saint
53 Favoring
54 Endowments
56 SWAYS
60 "L'etat ___ moi": Louis XIV
61 Tailor-made
63 Bruises
64 Make mad
65 "Come Back to ___"
66 Mil. schools
68 Nimbus
71 Former Russ. state
73 Los ___, CA
75 The Pepsi Challenge, e.g.
80 "Man and Superman" man
81 ABS
83 Carol opener
84 Pineta, e.g.
86 Gets one's goat
88 Mary in "Red Dust"
89 Altar girls
90 L.A.'s 40th mayor
93 Take the rubber
95 Demeanor
96 Curling cry
97 AD
101 Vain flowers?
104 Saying
105 Julie in "Show Boat" (1951)
108 Persuades
109 Ramble
111 With dance or dunk
115 EVENT
117 GUS
119 Always
120 Canal for Sal
121 German pronoun
122 Nerve, of a sort
123 Bill rolls
124 Thurber's "The Years with ___"
125 Boxer and pug
126 Orgs.

DOWN

1 Tip one's hat
2 Tishri follows it
3 Sorrento coin
4 Generic Jacuzzi
5 Finn or fin follower
6 Enola Gay, for one
7 Plaza Hotel girl
8 "Duke of ___": Chandler
9 Removes the reins
10 Works like Donatello
11 Portage craft
12 Day wear for knights
13 Coquette
14 Unnerve
15 Way out
16 1996 Fishburne film
17 G-men
19 Trifling talk
23 Napoleon's sister
25 George IV, once
31 Naysayer
33 Little one: Suffix
34 PRESS
35 Nosferatu features
36 Butler's belle
37 Bogey tracker
38 Compete in America's Cup
40 Stairstep part
41 Invert a pencil
42 Ease ender
46 Floatable woods
47 Rossini's "Le Comte ___"
49 BRAD
51 Mauna ___
52 Flattened at the poles
53 Canoodle
55 Mysore Mr.
57 "___ Teenage Werewolf" (1957)
58 Proof abbr.
59 Northern Ireland
62 Metal molds
67 ___ anglais (English horn)
69 Stage-actress Hagen
70 Pest-control targets
71 Ogress
72 It may get rattled
74 Cotton Sta.
76 Pose a query
77 ¿Dónde ___? (Where are they?)
78 Marcus Aurelius, e.g.
79 Celine Dion song
80 Impudence
81 Thrice: Rx
82 Ike's ex
85 Meal
87 Bartender, at times
90 Concerns
91 Colorado NHLers, for short
92 Stole
94 "Love ___ Around": Troggs
97 Chester A. Riley's friend
98 Emanated
99 Strong-arms
100 "___ Fables"
102 Allude
103 Mild Macanudo
105 Once again
106 "___ Zapata!" (1952)
107 Like Glenfiddich
110 Three of a kind
112 Oceans or mountains
113 Related
114 Advanced sci. degrees
116 The 24 in 24/7
118 Flapper's fashion item

49 CHAT WITH A COBBLER   by Frances Hansen
Is the cobbler a heel? You be the judge.

ACROSS

1 Carpenter's tool
5 Marine map
10 Venetian blind part
14 ___ d'art
19 Paris suburb
20 Maris or Moore
21 ___ Sad, Serbia
22 Wanders around
23 "Like ___ in June—hoists sail . . .: Shak.
24 Eat away
25 "Mourning Becomes Electra" role
26 "Sing, Sing, Sing" singer
27 **"You look overworked. Where's your help?"**
31 Coast or penguin
32 Soissons summer
33 Contemptible
34 River isle
35 Say "I do"
38 Pottery oven
39 ___ Broadway
42 "Endymion" poet
45 "___, I'm Adam"
46 Widow's donation
47 Ice sheet
48 **"The one called Gillie?"**
52 "Vissi d'___": Puccini
53 On the qui vive
54 High ways
55 Raise on high
56 Cognac co.
57 Clare of "Bleak House"
58 Scar had a black one
59 Poetic praise from 42 Across
60 **"The one with the annoying habit?"**
69 Grandma's hair pad
70 "The Naked Truth" heroine
71 Like no-see-ums
72 Crusher of "Star Trek: TNG"
73 Once over lightly
76 Redman in "The Stand"
77 Come to
80 Fit of petulance
81 **"Couldn't you make him stop?"**
86 Venture capital
87 Emulate Niobe
88 Ankylosaur feature
89 Irene from Greece
90 "King Kong" studio
91 Pile up
92 Robbe-Grillet's birthplace
93 Suffix for "fil" or "imper"
94 Huntz of the Bowery Boys
95 Gear tooth
96 In the buff
99 **"Where's Gillie now?"**
107 Jubilate
108 Last name in spydom
109 Loos or Louise
110 "Ben-Hur" costume designer
111 Championship
112 Sherman Hemsley sitcom
113 Edible mushroom
114 Comical Kett
115 Loosened up
116 Dole out
117 Dagwood's "SKNXX-X"
118 Sunbeams

DOWN

1 Basque word for "merry"
2 Country home near Elbrus
3 Polyp, e.g.
4 Surround with flowers
5 Bureau type
6 Dike, Eunomia, and Irene
7 Balanchine ballet
8 Salon redress
9 IMAX film
10 High-hat
11 "Casablanca" actor
12 All agog
13 Sheet-metal worker
14 Esther Summerson, e.g.
15 Nonmetallic element
16 Pokey
17 Jane Austin book
18 Ivan the Terrible, e.g.
28 Goldie in "The First Wives Club"
29 Physicist Enrico
30 Bigwig, for short
35 Created
36 Month before Nisan
37 Hit the roof
38 Foil-wrapped candy
39 "Eugene Onegin" contralto
40 Umpire's cry
41 "Dogs"
42 Packsaddle packsack
43 Spooky
44 ___ in the right direction
45 SE Asian peninsula
46 Eeyore's creator
47 Some spyhoppers
49 Attacked
50 Authentic
51 Make more mauve
57 Yoga position
58 Gabon president (1961–67)
59 Portents
61 Musty
62 Shoe part
63 Still abed
64 Chow
65 Take an oath
66 Come clean
67 Girl protected by Don Juan
68 Will in "New Port South"
73 Standing open
74 Icky stuff
75 Concerning
77 "When you ___ a tulip . . ."
78 Octopus octet
79 Anchor bend, e.g.
80 Trivia, to Andy Capp
82 "Super!"
83 Terrier type
84 Flat-bottomed boat
85 Swiftly
91 Brought to a standstill
92 Jersey, for one
93 Take a deep breath
94 Berry in "Swordfish"
95 Emoticon symbol
96 Pronounce
97 Main artery
98 Daft
99 Festive occasion
100 Any of the iris family
101 Soup-to-___
102 Plucky
103 Smithfield products
104 Party to the deal
105 "Catalan Landscape" painter
106 Afternoon receptions

50 ROLLER COASTER by Nancy Nicholson Joline
"Wheeeeee!"

ACROSS

1 Swathes
7 Made sense
13 Conjecture
20 Consumed
21 Big Bertha, for one
22 Coach
23 Snare
24 "Our Love Is ___ Stay"
25 Lively, musically
26 Wreath decorations
28 Like Lamb's pig
30 Disappointments
31 Muscovite princes
32 Combat missions
34 Stretch out
38 Takes in
39 Via Veneto locale
40 Limo alternative
43 Like a studio couch
45 Exhaust
49 Example
51 Scouting mission
52 Faux pas
54 Young dumb girl
55 Do a masseur's job
56 Fusses over fatuously
57 Sea duck
59 Most down-at-heel
61 Confess
63 Sluices
64 Like the ERA
67 "The Hudsucker Proxy" star
69 Buckle up
73 Chocolate dogs
75 Ackbar and Piett of "Star Wars"
80 "___ I'm mistaken . . ."
81 Stephen King fans
84 Sea or sea fan
85 Neighbor of Windsor Castle
86 Over
87 Sixties dress style
88 Bibb and Boston
92 Word with case or paper
93 Agnes Scott or Joe
95 Has high tea
96 "___ Song": Ringo Starr
97 In a NY minute

99 Only horse to beat Man o' War
100 Life-size cardboard cutouts
104 "Dwelt a miner forty-___ . . ."
106 Sheraton patron
110 Anne in "Rhoda"
111 Pink Lady ingredient
116 Support
118 Stringed sculpture
120 Slippery one
121 Cat claw
122 It brings some to tears
123 Overcome
124 Where runoffs occur
125 Traveller and Trigger
126 Albany, to New York City

DOWN

1 Hard to understand
2 Indian royal
3 Memo abbr.
4 Fille's father
5 Play
6 Assumes
7 Stick
8 Sunday finest
9 S. Lee or A. Lee
10 Civil-rights leader Medgar
11 Artoo-___
12 Hoo-ha
13 Place in position
14 Breakfast-bar sight
15 Inveighs against
16 He's not one to talk
17 ___ the finish
18 Put in writing
19 "Antony and Cleopatra" role
27 Amendment defeaters

29 Emulate a pole dancer
33 They're found in marmalade
34 Escapades
35 Musical of 1919
36 Figure in 28 Across
37 Retrieve a file
40 Franklin memorial
41 Central Park's 843
42 Exert full strength
44 Frisée and witloof
46 Needle point
47 Canadian gas
48 Like Joel's girl
50 Fusses
52 Super 8
53 Politically incorrect suffix
56 It ends in Oct.
57 Spurious
58 Like a dunce cap
60 More than eras

62 Path for a Horatio Alger hero
65 It may be poison
66 Pessimistic
68 "Scrubs" roles
69 Adds to the fire
70 Pay
71 Casino coin collectors
72 Big top
74 Sound
76 Cost increase
77 Dodge of the '80s
78 "Losing Isaiah" star
79 Road hazard
82 Bouvier ___ Flandres dog
83 Involved
86 In unison
89 Loosen Mary Janes
90 Foldaway
91 Crown covers
93 Chaplin prop
94 Expanded

98 Lola and Lorelei
101 Moistens
102 Eradicate
103 Zibeline
105 Storms
106 "___ Tonight": K.C. & the Sunshine Band
107 Organ-transplant org.
108 "James Joyce" biographer
109 "And to say ___ more.": Shak.
112 Bonkers
113 "What's the big ___?"
114 Peachy
115 "Broadway's in Fashion" artist
117 "Sprechen ___ Deutsch?"
119 Eugene O'Neill play

ANSWERS

AAA
TUBBS
MADCAPS
PAKISTANI
EYEOPENER
CANTO NRA
STARLET
OPTED
ESO

FOREWORD

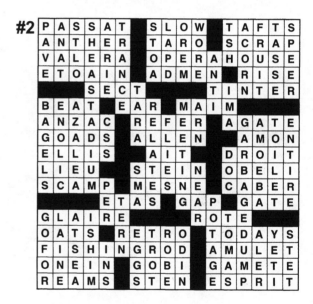

#1

W	O	R	S	E		S	A	D	D	L	E		M	E	O	W
I	S	A	A	C		O	B	R	I	E	N		A	Q	U	A
F	L	I	G	H	T	F	O	O	T	E	D		R	U	N	G
E	O	N		O	R	A	L	S			S	O	L	A	C	E
			I	B	I	S	E	S		D	E	L	E	S		
A	P	T		H	U	E	S		L	E	R	O	Y			
F	A	R	M	A	N	D	H	A	M	M	E	R		B	O	S
F	R	E	E	Z	E		L	E	I	F		L	O	R	E	
E	L	A	T	E		P	A	I	R	S		T	O	X	I	C
C	O	T	S		B	A	R	B		S	E	C	T	O	R	
T	R	Y		F	A	C	E	I	N	T	H	E	H	O	L	E
		J	A	N	E	T		E	R	I	N		P	E	T	
A	D	H	O	C		D	E	M	E	A	N					
S	E	E	S	T	O		I	D	L	E	S		S	A	T	
I	N	C	H		F	E	T	C	H	A	S	K	E	T	C	H
A	S	H	E		F	L	O	R	A	L		I	D	A	H	O
N	E	E	D		S	O	N	O	M	A		T	U	B	E	R

#2

P	A	S	S	A	T		S	L	O	W		T	A	F	T	S
A	N	T	H	E	R		T	A	R	O		S	C	R	A	P
V	A	L	E	R	A		O	P	E	R	A	H	O	U	S	E
E	T	O	A	I	N		A	D	M	E	N		R	I	S	E
		S	E	C	T					T	I	N	T	E	R	
B	E	A	T		E	A	R		M	A	I	M				
A	N	Z	A	C		R	E	F	E	R		A	G	A	T	E
G	O	A	D	S		A	L	L	E	N			A	M	O	N
E	L	L	I	S			A	I	T		D	R	O	I	T	
L	I	E	U		S	T	E	I	N		O	B	E	L	I	
S	C	A	M	P		M	E	S	N	E		C	A	B	E	R
			E	T	A	S		G	A	P		G	A	T	E	
G	L	A	I	R	E			R	O	T	E					
O	A	T	S		R	E	T	R	O		T	O	D	A	Y	S
F	I	S	H	I	N	G	R	O	D		A	M	U	L	E	T
O	N	E	I	N		G	O	B	I		G	A	M	E	T	E
R	E	A	M	S		S	T	E	N		E	S	P	R	I	T

#3

A	L	A	M	E	D	A		A	D	A	M		A	L	T	O
D	E	C	I	B	E	L		V	I	N	O		S	E	E	D
I	T	I	S	B	E	T	T	E	R	T	O		S	A	N	D
T	O	D	D			H	U	R	T	S		M	A	N	S	E
			E	A	T	E	R	S			S	U	I	T	E	S
H	A	V	E	L	O	A	F	E	D	A	N	D	L	O	S	T
A	V	I	D	L	Y			A	B	I	D	E				
L	A	S	S	O		B	I	G	T	O	P		R	A	V	I
L	I	T		T	H	A	N	N	E	V	E	R		R	E	D
S	L	A	P		O	B	T	U	S	E		E	B	O	N	Y
		L	A	M	E	R			A	N	I	M	A	L		
T	O	H	A	V	E	L	O	A	F	E	D	A	T	A	L	L
U	N	I	T	E	D		S	I	L	E	N	T				
R	E	N	T	S		M	A	L	T	A		E	I	R	E	
B	I	T	E		J	A	M	E	S	T	H	U	R	B	E	R
O	D	E	R		A	L	O	E		E	A	R	N	I	N	G
T	A	D	S		W	I	S	P		S	W	I	S	S	E	S

#4

J	A	P	A	N		C	R	A	P	S		A	G	I	L	E
A	B	A	S	E		R	A	B	A	T		N	A	V	E	S
N	O	N	E	T		E	V	E	R	Y		A	V	A	S	T
E	D	D			O	D	E	T	S			T	E	N	S	E
T	E	A	L	I	K	I	S	S	E	D	Y	O	U			
			O	N	I	T				R	O	M	P	E	D	
	B	L	A	D	E	S		L	E	A	K	Y		C	A	B
H	A	I	T	I			P	A	L	M	E		B	A	N	E
U	N	C	H	A	I	N	E	D	M	A	L	L	A	R	D	Y
G	A	T	E		N	O	E	L	S			A	N	T	E	S
O	N	O		A	D	O	R	E		S	E	T	Z	E	R	
	A	R	A	M	I	S				T	I	E	A			
			H	A	V	E	E	I	D	E	R	R	I	G	H	T
A	N	D	E	S			A	L	I	V	E			O	A	R
L	E	E	R	S		A	T	O	N	E		F	R	O	Z	E
S	H	A	N	E		D	I	V	A	N		E	B	S	E	N
O	I	L	E	D		O	N	E	R	S		W	I	E	L	D

#5

```
J I B E S  ■ B E C C A ■ H U S S Y
O N E N O  ■ A K R O N ■ I N A W E
S T A T S  ■ L E A D S ■ M I M E S
H E N R A T I S S E ■ L O R C A ■
■ G P A ■ R H O S ■ D E M O O R E
I R O N ■ A A U ■ P A X ■ Y O S T
T A L C ■ D I T H E R ■ F A K I R
S L E E V E ■ A N Y ■ I L E N E
■ ■ E S A O R A L E S ■ ■ ■
A N W A R ■ M R S ■ ■ S T E W E D
L E A R Y ■ A S H A R P ■ A H S O
F A R M ■ U S O ■ S U R ■ R I C H
A R E Y E R S ■ M I N I ■ P T A
■ B A N A L ■ J O N I T C H E L L
D E G A S ■ R O D I N ■ R O L L E
D E L V E ■ E V E N T ■ O N I O N
T R E Y S ■ M I M E O ■ W E E P S
```

#6

```
F O R M ■ ■ B A S H ■ ■ P E A K S
A D I O S ■ O L E O ■ G A R N E T
N O S T A L G I A S S O L I K E A
G R E E C E ■ A M I C O ■ C A P T
■ ■ ■ T H R U ■ A N A ■ ■ R E E
■ L E S S O N I N G R A M M A R
F I R ■ ■ Y I N ■ ■ F R A U ■ ■
E V E N T ■ T D S ■ ■ I N F R A
B E C A U S E Y O U C A N F I N D
■ S T I L E ■ S P A ■ A S T I R
■ ■ V I E R ■ ■ O S S ■ E L Y
■ T H E P R E S E N T T E N S E
B R O ■ ■ C O D ■ S U M O ■ ■
L I R E ■ M A N I A ■ P I N T A S
A N D T H E P A S T P E R F E C T
K E E N A N ■ T O M E ■ S A C R E
E S S A Y ■ ■ A N O N ■ ■ T H E N
```

#7

```
M I D S T ■ S C R A P ■ T U N A ■
I R A Q I ■ T O U C H ■ O N I C E
R E R U N ■ A N N U L ■ S I G M A
■ L E T S G E T T O G E T H E R
C R E A S E ■ S E X I E S T ■ ■
O I N K ■ R A G ■ L E N D ■ C P A
W O E ■ D I S M A Y S ■ C L O G
■ ■ B O O T E E ■ S P O U S E
S E E Y O U I N S E P T E M B E R
C A P E R S ■ O P I A T E ■ ■
O C H S ■ R A P I E R S ■ J A W
T H E ■ A D E N ■ C D T ■ T E S H
■ M A R I T A L ■ T R A S H Y
M E E T M E I N S T L O U I S ■
C O R A L ■ T I A R A ■ B L I M P
S N A R E ■ L A T E R ■ L O C A L
■ S L I T ■ E S S E S ■ E R A T O
```

#8

```
M A A M ■ A S L A N T ■ A D A P T
A L V A ■ L A T V I A ■ M E L E E
G L E N N A N D A N N M I L L E R
S A R G E S ■ ■ A D A ■ ■ E L M
■ L A L A ■ S A O ■ E N E M Y ■
R O G E R A N D D E M I M O O R E
O N E S ■ W I D O W ■ C O P O U T
B E D ■ P E P ■ M E G ■ T E P E E
■ ■ R A S P B E R R I E S ■ ■
D E B A R ■ Y E T ■ E S S ■ T A P
O R A C L E ■ R E B E L ■ B E L L
G E N E A N D G R A C E K E L L Y
■ D R Y E R ■ S H E ■ I L L S
P E A ■ M O I ■ ■ I N L A W S
S P I K E A N D B R E N D A L E E
S E D A N ■ E E R I E R ■ M I L E
T E S T S ■ D O O D L E ■ Y E L P
```

#9

```
B U F F O ■ A B A F T ■ S C R A M
A P R O N ■ C A N O E ■ N O O S E
S T A R S ■ C A I R N ■ A W O K E
S O U G H T U S ■ F O U G H T U S
I N D O O R S ■ P E N N ■ E S S E
■ ■ R Y E ■ R I S K E R ■ ■
T A S T E ■ L E T ■ N O D O F F
R A T E ■ P R O P ■ L O N ■ N E E
A R I D ■ R O Y ■ L E W ■ S E L L
C O N ■ T O M ■ B E A N ■ H A L O
I N G R I D ■ M A O ■ D Y L A N
■ A M U L E T ■ A L I ■ ■
S O O N ■ C A S H ■ M O N T A G E
C A U G H T U S ■ T A U G H T U S
A R T I E ■ R I V E N ■ B E R E T
L E G E R ■ E L A N D ■ A R I S E
A D O R E ■ L Y N D A ■ T E A S E
```

#10

```
T A C O ■ G O L E M ■ R A K I N G
A J A R ■ A L I B I ■ U N I Q U E
T A M E ■ T E N O N ■ S E C U R E
A X E ■ G O O D N I G H T K I S S
■ ■ T I E R S ■ B O O ■ ■ T E E
S A O N E ■ W A I T F O R ■ ■
C L A D ■ D R I N K O F W A T E R
A C H Y ■ R A N G E ■ N E H R U
R O E ■ F E W ■ ■ H A S ■ E O N
A V A I L ■ I B S E N ■ I B I S
B E D T I M E S T O R Y ■ O R C A
■ ■ S T A Y O U T ■ S T O A T
A S P ■ G E L ■ A S I A N ■ ■
S T U F F E D A N I M A L ■ X T C
P I L E O N ■ T A C I T ■ E Z R A
I N P A R T ■ E M O T E ■ L O A F
N E S T E A ■ D E N Y S ■ M O P E
```

#11

```
L E V O N . S P R A T . D O L E S
I N I G O . A R E N A . O P A R T
B E S E T . M E L E E . M E N S A
E R I E S . O L I N . B I N D E R
L O T S O F A U C T I O N S .
. . A N D . M R I . T I C
F I S H E R . E L O P E . P O N E
E N T E R . A R E A . L A V A
S C O R E S O F B A L L G A M E S
T O R O . E B R O . I N A N E
A M E N . W E I R D . A G E N T S
L E D . W E S . E S L
. P I L E S O F C A R P E T S
R E C A L L . A S I A . A L L O W
O V E R T . A T A L L . S E A T O
M A N S E . L I K E D . P A T I O
A N T E D . B E A D S . S T E E P
```

#12

```
T A C O . N E N E . A Q U A . E D A M
A R A M . A R U T . G U M P . S A L E
T A L E N T I S C H E A P E R T H A N
. C L O A K . H O S T . O A S I S
T R U E R S . A E R . R O B O T
S A L T W H A T S E P A R A T E S
A B U . A P T . B R I N K S . O E R
R I S E S . O L E . E N O L . K Y L E
. C L A R E N C E . A R I O S E
A T A L E N T E D I N D I V I D U A L
M A L A D Y . O V E R L A N D
M O O T . T E R R . D E I . D O F F S
O S O . F I N E S T . N A S . I L O
. F R O M T H E S U C C E S S F U L
. A R E S O . A S H . V A T T E D
M E R C K . N A V E . L E R O Y
O N E I S A L O T O F H A R D W O R K
R Y E S . N E R O . O O Z E . E N N A
T A F T . G A S P . R E E D . D E A N
```

#13

```
J I G S A W . C O T T A . S P O O K S
E N R O B E . E L I H U . C L I P O N
S C U B A S . M A N I C . H A L I T E
T A M E S T . E V E N T . U N I A T E
E S P I E S . N I S E I . M O N T E Z
R E S T R I C T . O R A N G E R Y
. . D O W N . A N O N
B U T C H E R R O A D S U N G L A S S
O S H E A . N I T R A T E . N A G E L
R U I N G . T H E M A . A T O N E
I R E N E . L E O T A R D . S T R O P
C Y L I N D E R M E N T A L H E A R T
. . E A S E . T I T O
M E L B L A N C . N E W S C A S T
I N U R E D . I D T A G . C L O S E R
A D R I A N . N I E U W . L E S S E E
S M I D G E . D A N D O . A U T U M N
M A N A U S . E N E R O . S T A R E D
A N G L E S . R A T E D . S H R E D S
```

#14

```
A S P S . A M P E R E . L I K E W O W
U C L A . R E A V E D . A B I L E N E
D I A N . B I P E D S . M A T I N E E
I F I G N O R A N C E . P R E S T O
T I N E A R . T O L D . A N I
. R E D I D . A S E C . H I T O N
L I S . A D E B T . S L A M M I N G
O N C E A Y E A R . S P O T O F T E A
R E A L M . L A B T E S T
I S B L I S S W H Y A R E N T M O R E
. C H I M E R A . R A D A R
S T A N D O U T S . C D P L A Y E R S
D E S P A T C H . P H O T O . R E T
A L A R M . K I R I . S A I N T
K E W . T I M S . T A R S A L
. P H E L P S . P E O P L E H A P P Y
I L O V E I T . E N D E A R . N A R C
C A L I S T A . S T A N C E . C R E E
E Y E L E T S . T O S S E D . E S S E
```

#15

```
G O F I S H . S A H A R A . S C R A M
A C A D I A . O N E M A N . O R A L E
U T T E R L Y D I S O R G A N I Z E D
G A T E S . O A T . S E E M . T O R I
E V E . A S S A I . R O B E R T A
D O R M A N T . N E W S I E R
. U R I . E A T N O . E I E I O
S H U F F L E D D E C K O F C A R D S
T E N T S . L O O N . D A H . R E T
E R E I . G E M S T O N E S . T A A L
A B S . L I V . I N A T . T A N T E
M A C H I N E I S O U T O F O R D E R
S L O A N . T E N S E . U N A
. R E G A T T A . S E I S M I C
L A N D S A T . L A B E L . A N O
A L A W . R O L E . L O W . G I S T S
S C R A M B L E D E G G S A N D H A M
S A C R E . L A N D A U . C A L I C O
O N S E T . S P A D E S . T W E E T S
```

#16

```
A W E S O M E . O M A R . J E E R A T
K A S H M I R . L A V A . A L B I N O
I N Q U I S I T I V E B U S Y B O D Y
N E S T S . T A G . R I C O . G A S
. S E R I O U S D A N G E R
S E N T I N E L . S I L L . A V A S T
A R I Z O N A . B U O Y . A V E N U E
I N T U N E . P L A N . A M E N D E D
D O S . U R A L . S P O I L E R S
. C L O S E S C R U T I N Y
P O T H O L E S . U I E S . L I E
U N H A N D S . P S S T . B E A U T S
S T I N G S . N A T E . P I T S T O P
S O N D E . N O L O . Q U A C K E R Y
. S U D D E N I M P U L S E
S N O . U M P S . O I L . T E S L A
C O L L A B O R A T E T O G E T H E R
A S E A S Y . O D E S . F A R E A S T
R E D S E A . S E X Y . F L A S H E S
```

#17

```
HASP  RACY  ARPA  MAYA
OMAR  ALEE  NEED  ALAN
LAGO  NARA  AFAR  CELT
THEDOCTORSCURE    AXES
        PIE  BAIT  MIR
STOWED  CORNER  LOOSE
PERON   COO   AVENGER
ACER  ALLKINDSOFILLS
SHORTCUT  BAREST  EAT
      YOU  INANY  TIP
FOE  RAISER  DRONEBEE
EXCEPTTHESHOCK   SARG
DECREES   ACA   STELA
SNEAD  ATWORK  SCORED
      SOB  IHAD  TEA
ETNA  OFDOCTORSBILLS
DRAB  OLIO  ABET  ZOOT
GIRL  SEEP  CAVE  OGPU
YOKE  TADS  KNIT  DYED
```

#18

```
WALES  SMARTEST  FEDS
EXILE  ERICIDLE  EXAM
DIVEREVELATION   ZANE
GARNERED   NAES   CIA
ELEANOR  SPYANTEATER
     ASI  TOE  ESTELLE
BESIDETHEPOT    TOYED
ABOVE  YAR  HADRON
TERESA  RNA  KAOS  HEP
ERRS  HUMANBEGS  LANA
STY  CALF  SLO  SQUINT
     EASEUP  UNS  UNTIE
MASTS   LEAREQUATION
ENTRAPS   SUR   URI
MAREBIOLOGY  IINSIST
OTO  ALPE  ORATORIO
POLY  ARACETOTHEFISH
ALLA  TOPPRIZE  SENSI
DESK  ENTAILED  TRAYS
```

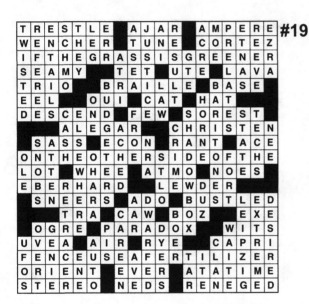

#19

```
TRESTLE  AJAR  AMPERE
WENCHER  TUNE  CORTEZ
IFTHEGRASSISGREENER
SEAMY  TET  UTE  LAVA
TRIO   BRAILLE   BASE
EEL  OUI  CAT  HAT
DESCEND  FEW  SOREST
    ALEGAR   CHRISTEN
SASS  ECON  RANT  ACE
ONTHEOTHERSIDEOFTHE
LOT  WHEE  ATMO  NOES
EBERHARD    LEWDER
SNEERS  ADO  BUSTLED
    TRA  CAW  BOZ  EXE
OGRE  PARADOX  WITS
UVEA  AIR  RYE  CAPRI
FENCEUSEAFERTILIZER
ORIENT  EVER  ATATIME
STEREO  NEDS  RENEGED
```

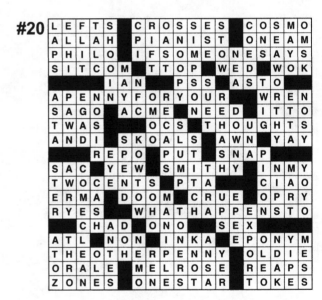

#20

```
LEFTS  CROSSES  COSMO
ALLAH  PIANIST  ONEAM
PHILO  IFSOMEONESAYS
SITCOM  TTOP  WED  WOK
    IAN   PSS   ASTO
APENNYFORYOUR   WREN
SAGO  ACME  NEED  ITTO
TWAS   OCS   THOUGHTS
ANDI  SKOALS  AWN  YAY
     REPO  PUT  SNAP
SAC  YEW  SMITHY  INMY
TWOCENTS  PTA   CIAO
ERMA  DOOM  CRUE  OPRY
RYES  WHATHAPPENSTO
    CHAD  ONO  SEX
ATL  NON  INKA  EPONYM
THEOTHERPENNY  OLDIE
ORALE  MELROSE  REAPS
ZONES  ONESTAR  TOKES
```

#21

```
GOODAT  PINE  FORSURE
ONLINE  ODIE  UNEATEN
TADPOLEKICK  SEAWALL
III  DELETE  OSU  HAI
TRES  IMA  PUPPYDAYS
   LESSOR  USO  ERNST
  SHADE  NOAM  TATE
STINGER  DIMS  PISTOL
KITTYNAP  REESE  SANE
IFS  CUBCLAW  CSA
PLOD  CELLO  LAMBSKIN
SENECA  LOOM  TEAPOTS
   AUDI  NLER  ALONE
APPLE  NED  LERNER
COLTSENSE  ABO  TAFT
CPA  PAT  FLUTES  CRO
OLIVIER  CALFCATCHER
RADIOED  CLEF  RANOUT
DRSEUSS  CANS  SYNODS
```

#22

```
HAST  LOTT  BAZ  SEGO
OREO  FURRY  AGO  URAL
POLITICSISWHEREBALD
INFLUX  OBOE  DRAT
    EGAD  ANDS  ORLONS
BIRD  TOLL  GOA  NENES
ITE  PERU  SIMBA  ICON
FATDISAGREEABLEMEN
ILIAC  LEON  YELP
DOESNT  SWANK  CLANGS
   TION  TUNE  ECOLE
TEACHAPRESIDENTHOW
CHAR  OGRES  FIRS  IVE
CORDS  SAC  RENO  STER
DULLES  YODA  ATOM
   YANK  URBS  INURED
TOACTONAPUBLICSTAGE
URDU  OOH  ILONA  TRAY
BEAR  PBA  DEPT  YENS
```

Crossword puzzle solutions.

#23

```
RAPS  GRIPS  MIMI   STA
ABUT  AUDIO  ODIN   PEN
BOLO  STEAM  LEND   EMT
BULKS SANE   DADO   EPA
ITSELF LOWE  SMOLDER
WREAK  SHAG  AROUSE
SEE  DREW  ERUPT  OPTS
TRAM ERROR TITAN
RITES RATES PER  WAR
OCELOT PITHY REMOTE
PAR LAG SHOOT AORTA
JOKER EDGAR SKID
SOSA EMBER ALEC ICY
PLANET IRAS LEARN
ADRENAL AIMS FRUGAL
TLC DRAT NOAH ESTEE
TIA IGGY BONER SIRE
ENS VEEP OCTET EMIR
REM ETRE WHALE TEES
```

#24

```
AREAS BACH PET IFSO
TELLA OGLE APE NITE
AMATI SHARPTON SEAR
NOBODYCANBEEXACTLY
OSHA SILLYME DST
OUR IDOS ELL OLMOS
ALAD DINO EAST SIVA
TETE OLIVETREE ACER
SEEYA SPUN CRATERS
LIKEMEEVENI
HAROLDI READ DANSE
OLAV ENSCONCED OTOE
OPIE ASTA YURI KHAN
HENNA ETS ASEC DRS
AND SOAPSUP GHEE
HAVETROUBLEDOINGIT
OONA TINPLATE NORSE
ARCS ELI ECRU OCEAN
KNEE RST TEES SHEWS
```

#25

```
RIGGED HAIR DRU TAB
EMERGE OMNI RON APE
GEORGEJEFFERSON LPS
RAD SPA MONEYMARKET
ENOS EIN ZIN MESA
TIMEANDAGAIN DEVISE
STEPPE ERG KOD TEX
EDA AUSTIN DOME
RIDER LIFEPRESERVER
ENIAC TNT OOF ANENT
FORTUNECOOKIE SORTS
INES GRANDE ROT
LES VOS OUT NOMAAM
ESTHER HARPERSFERRY
GRIT AUK NUT AMER
GLAMOURGIRL FRI OTT
ROI ESSENCEOFEMERIL
ART REO TAIL ARSENE
BYS SSN OSSA METROS
```

#26

```
HST ACE SMILER SKEW
THEPROS OCTAVE LAVA
TOELESS PGTWENTYSIX
PEDANT ASI RAN ETE
IDLES LSU TOAMAN
TWENTYGALLONHATS
UPA GPO NEO EERIE
BARNUM VPS HIS ARC
OPENSEA MON DIET
ONCLOUDEIGHTEEN
TELE ERE ADSORBS
AGE GED TNT ABIDED
NOSIR IRR ATE OED
CATCHEIGHTYWINKS
MADEDO OKS EAVES
APE ERR CAY ENLIST
THEFABEIGHT ATTACHE
TIRO ANOMIE STAYOUT
EDER YENTAS PET NNE
```

#27

```
AMOS LIENS GLOMS ALAS
RIGA INDIA AESOP SABU
CELINEDINO TALIASHIER
ONEDIGIT PESO CIRCLE
TER JAIME ZETA
HADIT ADESTE REMEMBER
OLIVIA ETHANCONE SELA
ILAY BERT UPEND TLC
SAN JIMMYCRATER ARTIE
THEMEDIA RIDER PREYED
SEWER HENRY RETAG
BAWLED PASSE BASERATE
ATALL BETTEMIDLER ROD
SAY SCONE NAST ABBA
ILED RONSLIVER ASYLUM
CEREMONY ODORED TREYS
POSE PILOT ARE
MACROS SATE TRAVERSE
ALBERTOGRE MARKIEPOTS
UTES INTER ABIES IMUS
DORS ESSES SAONE CEDE
```

#28

```
HALS ACAT TEASE SEAM
ALEC AMISH SANER ESSO
PAAR RENTE ESTER TAIL
IFIWEREABETTERARTIST
BON EASE TOE
IDBEAPAINTERIFIWERE
ORALS RINDS NICE ALF
DICE FORKS BEDE LATER
ISH AIDES PAYOFF LINE
CHARLES BURRO UPLOAD
IAN ABETTER SEA
PASSED GENTS MSCHULZ
OGLE SHORES FLEES SOA
SLING AUNT GOULD CURL
HOE OMIT BUNCO SHADE
WRITERIDWRITENOVELS
MAI ARID TEN
IMNOTSOIMACARTOONIST
LOON TRAPS NOONE LOAD
ELUL EDGES CARES LUXE
DENY ROONE ERAS ERIN
```

Crossword puzzle solutions.

#29

```
D E C A | T R O T S | D A B A T | C R A W
A V O W | H E C H E | A G R E E | L I T E
T A C K M A S T E R | R A I S E | A C H E
A G A | O R E | T A N N I C | D U N K E D
A C T I | T A I | O I N K S | S T Y N E
O B O I S T | I M N O T | T I D E O V E R
R O L L T O P D E C K | A R G O N N E
G R A D | L A S S O | M A N G O | N A P
E V E N | E R O D E S | E T A L
L I B | E D G E | F L O R I D | L A U R A
A D A G I O | L E A D M E N | B A R R O N
P E C A N | S E T T E E | G M E N | E N S
S A K I | C I P H E R | A H A T
E L I | D O N H O | F I O N A | R A S P
N E O N G A S | H U C K Y V O I C E D
E S T R O G E N | T O N E R | E L A T E S
C O H A N | S T R A Y | H A I | I D E S
O N E S E C | T A T T O O | N A V | D I T
L O S E | A C U R A | M U C K M E L O N S
A M U R | R I C E R | E S T E E | A U T O
B A N S | P O K E S | N E A R S | G T O S
```

#30

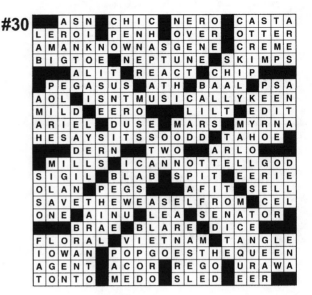

```
A S N | C H I C | N E R O | C A S T A
L E R O I | P E N H | O V E R | O T T E R
A M A N K N O W N A S G E N E | C R E M E
B I G T O E | N E P T U N E | S K I M P S
A L I T | R E A C T | C H I P
P E G A S U S | A T H | B A A L | P S A
A O L | I S N T M U S I C A L L Y K E E N
M I L D | E E R O | L I L T | E D I T
A R I E L | D U S E | M A R S | M Y R N A
H E S A Y S I T S S O O D D | T A H O E
D E R N | T W O | A R L O
M I L L S | I C A N N O T T E L L G O D
S I G I L | B L A B | S P I T | E E R I E
O L A N | P E G S | A F I T | S E L L
S A V E T H E W E A S E L F R O M | C E L
O N E | A I N U | L E A | S E N A T O R
B R A E | B L A R E | D I C E
F L O R A L | V I E T N A M | T A N G L E
I O W A N | P O P G O E S T H E Q U E E N
A G E N T | A C O R | R E G O | U R A W A
T O N T O | M E D O | S L E D | E E R
```

#31

```
T R A C T | S T A G E D | S L O V A K I A
R E T R O | H A L I T E | N I N E P I N S
A T L A N T A R A V E S | U T T E R N U T
D I E M | A R O S E | A G E | O G R E
E R A | S T E T | S E A L | T E N S E R
R E S A L E S | D W A R F S | H A S
S E T T O | E A R M A R K E T | P A S
T E S T | S Y N E | A I R | D A R T
A R F | S H O A T | E N A | D E F A R G E
L E A P | A G R I | D I N A | A C T O N
A S S E T H O U N D | A D M O U T H I N G
B I T E R | M E R E | A M I S | A N N E
A D E L I N E | D A N | N O S E S | G E L
M E N S | O T O | G N A T | E R I C
A S S | L E A K H O U S E | R E S E T
D O N | S O N I C S | S T E L L A R
A L M O N D | E S S E | S P A N | E R E
L I A M | E S S | N A T A L | T E N S
E F R I E N D S | O L D F A C E T Y P E S
R E I N D E E R | F A E R I E | A N I S E
T R A I T O R S | F O D O R S | D E N T S
```

#32

```
F E S S | S O D A | H I S S A T | C L A M
E L E M | I R A N | A N T H R O | L I M A
D O M E | D O W N U N D E R P O P O V E R
O P I A T E | B A L K | R E S | E W E R S
R E P R O S | E N T I C E D | B A N D I T
A R R | I T A R | R E A | A Y N | I G O
O G L E S | C A S T O F F T U R N O N
F I D O | P A R A | S W O R E T O
O D E O N | P E R M S | E R A | S L A Y
R E F F E D | A B O U T | I N S H A P E
E N C | H O E D O W N W I N D U P | U P A
S T O R I E D | S U E M E | B E R G E R
T I N E | I T O | P E A R L | C O H A N
C A S S A V A | G O O D | S I R S
R E S T S T O P O U T G O | S E D A N
E N T | P E N | N O R | S E M I | C A B
C R U C E S | A L T O I S T | I N C O M E
R O T O R | S L O | R E A R | T E A P O T
O U T B A C K C O L D F R O N T | P O E T
S T E R | B E A N I E | A D E E | T U B E
S E R A | C E N S E R | N E E D | S T A R
```

#33

```
S T R A W | N A T A L | S O I L | P R E S
T R A C E | A L I B I | C I T Y | R O T H
Y O U H A V E B E E N S E L E C T E D T O
X Y L E N E | S L E E P Y | E A T S U P
L E O | A R T | U T E
A T T E N D O U R F R E E S E M I N A R
B R I N E | S T E R | R P M | S T E P
O U T G O | S L I P S | E I N | I O N A
W E L L S H O W Y O U H O W T O L O W E R
D E E | U N I | N E W | W I N N E R
D R A M A S | A L B E I T
A S K F O R | R E D | A S S | E S P
Y O U R C A R I N S U R A N C E R A T E S
A N N E | H O D | S C O L D | A M A R A
H O T S | T E C | B I B I | N E R D S
W E H A V E A H O T S T O C K I S S U E
W W I | I W A | X I I
S T E A L S | F L E X E S | T A U G H T
T H A T S H O U L D I N T E R E S T Y O U
L A V E | N A M E | E Y E O N | P A R E R
O D E R | U S E R | D A W N S | S H O R N
```

#34

```
W I N K | C O B S | H A S T O | A B B O T
E L I A | A P O P | I R W I N | P R U N E
B E N H U R R A Y | G R A C E | P E R I L
S T A N D P A T | T H A N K S A L A T T E
D O H | E A S Y | S P E D
S N I P E R | C A M E | O M A R | P I P E
M A C A R T H U R P A R K A Y | S A N E R
O V E N S | U R L | S I R S | S E N D E R
G E T A | S T A Y S | V A S S A R | E W E
C H E | T O M E I | S T A B B E D
A C H I C K E N I N E V E R Y P A T E
L O R E T T A | L O R A X | R E L
O R E | M O N R O E | A N T E S | O M O O
S T A L E R | A U R A | I R S | A N O L D
E A T I N | F I R S T C L A S S M E L E E
S E E S | H E N S | H A L S | T A Y L O R
T O A D | I L S A | C O Z
M A N E T T O M A N E T | N A M E D R O P
A R E N T | R A N A T | C A N A D I A N S
C N O T E | A N K L E | E P I C | E R M A
H O N O R | S E A L S | O A T H | M E E T
```

#35

M	E	M	O	S		P	A	I	L		G	A	F	F		T	A	L	K	S
I	N	P	U	T		A	S	T	O		A	R	A	B		A	D	I	E	U
B	E	S	T	I	N	S	H	O	W		M	E	R	I	T	B	A	D	G	E
			W	R	O	T	E		B	A	B	A	R		H	O	P			
E	S	C	A	P	E	E		P	O	L	L	S		B	R	O	T	H	E	R
A	E	R	I	E	S		T	H	R	E	E		R	O	U	S	S	E	A	U
T	R	O	T	S		I	R	O	N	C	R	O	S	S		I	S	M		
I	B	I	S		G	N	A	T				N	T	H		P	E	S	T	O
N	I	X		C	O	R	D	O	N	B	L	E	U		F	O	R	M	E	R
G	A	D		O	B	O	E		E	R	I	S		D	O	L	L	A	R	S
		E	B	O	L	A		H	U	N		A	L	L	E	N				

#36

L	O	P	E	D		M	O	A	T		S	A	G	A		U	S	A	G	E
I	R	E	N	E		E	L	L	A		P	L	U	S		N	A	V	E	L
M	O	R	O	N		R	E	A	L		R	E	A	P		C	L	A	N	K
I	N	F	L	A	T	I	O	N	I	S	A	S	V	I	O	L	E	N	T	

#37

F	A	R		I	C	E	S	A		S	A	L	A		P	L	O	T	S
A	D	A		S	T	A	G	E	R		T	N	U	T		R	O	N	E	E
B	A	L	L	O	T	B	O	X	C	H	O	I	C	E		O	V	E	R	T

#38

W	I	L	B	U	R		A	S	T	O		K	P	S		S	A	C	R	O
A	V	E	R	N	O		R	A	I	N	O	U	T	S		E	T	H	E	R
R	E	D	A	C	T		C	H	E	E	C	H	A	N	D	C	H	A	N	G

#39

O	D	E	S	S	A		A	C	E	D		S	P	O	O	R		E	G	O
R	E	B	U	T	S		V	A	N	E		P	A	T	N	A		L	E	V
I	L	O	V	E	B	E	I	N	G	M	A	R	R	I	E	D		E	N	E

#40

M	A	H	A	L		S	P	A	T		B	A	N	J	O		H	A	G	S
A	L	I	N	E		E	L	L	E		I	C	I	E	R		A	B	I	T
W	A	L	T	E	R	W	A	L	L		D	U	C	A	T		M	O	V	E

(Completed crossword solution grids #35–#40)

Crossword Puzzles

#47

M	A	N	G	Y		C	O	P	T	E	R		I	C	E		C	B	E	R
A	G	O	R	A		A	R	A	R	A	T		D	O	D		O	R	L	E
V	E	T	E	R	I	N	A	R	I	A	N		A	L	A		U	E	L	E
	R	E	A	D	S		T	A	B		T	H	U	M	B	N	A	I	L	
	T	B	A		O	D	E		G	E	O	M		A	S	K				
P	E	D	I	A	T	R	I	C	I	A	N		N	O	R	E	L	L		
N	O	M	E	R	C	Y		S	A	N	G		I	N	B	L	O	O	M	
I	L	I	A	D		M	B	A		D	A	D		S	T	A		O	N	E
C	A	L	L		A	B	E	L	E			U	L	T		D	O	S	E	S
E	R	E		B	A	R		N	I	T	R	O		T	O	P	E	R	S	
			C	A	B	L	E	T	V	S	H	O	W	H	O	S	T			
D	E	F	A	M	E		F	O	Y	L	E		B	A	N		C	I	T	
A	M	O	O	N		D	T	S		A	P	I	N	G		B	O	N	A	
N	E	R		E	S	E		S	E	G		R	D	S		R	E	C	U	R
G	E	T	S	S	E	T		C	A	S	E		E	Y	E	S	O	R	E	
	R	E	H	I	R	E		S	H	O	E	S	A	L	E	S	M	A	N	
	P	E	A		C	O	C	O		T	E	L		R	O	E				
F	A	I	R	C	A	T	C	H		T	N	T		B	R	A	G	A		
O	D	A	I		T	I	E		P	S	Y	C	H	I	A	T	R	I	S	T
C	O	N	F		O	V	A		T	E	P	E	E	S		E	E	R	I	E
I	S	O	F		M	E	N		C	A	E	S	A	R		D	R	D	R	E

#48

D	E	L	H	I		B	E	E	F		S	C	A	T		J	E	F	F
O	L	I	O	S		P	O	L	A	R		C	A	R	E		A	X	L	E
F	U	R	T	H	E	R	M	O	R	E		U	N	M	A	R	R	I	E	D
F	L	A	T		L	A	B	I	L	E		L	O	O	S	E		T	D	S
			U	N	I	T	E	S		S	U	P	E	R	E	G	O			
F	O	R	B	E	S	T	R	E	S	U	L	T	S			E	F	R	E	M
A	H	A		G	E	L		A	P	E	S		B	O	N	F	I	R	E	
N	A	D	I	A		E	L	O	I			P	A	R	T	I	S	A	N	
G	R	A	N	T	S		O	B	L	I	Q	U	E	L	Y		C	E	S	T
S	A	R	T	O	R	I	A	L		W	E	L	T	S		I	R	E		
			E	R	I	N		A	C	A	D	S		A	U	R	A			
S	S	R		G	A	T	O	S		T	A	S	T	E	T	E	S	T		
S	H	A	W		T	O	L	E	R	A	T	E	S		A	D	E	S	T	E
A	R	B	O	R	E	T	A		I	R	K	S		A	S	T	O	R		
S	E	R	V	E	R	S		H	A	H	N		W	I	N		A	I	R	
S	W	E	E	P		G	A	V	E	A	S	S	I	S	T	A	N	C	E	
			N	A	R	C	I	S	S	I		P	H	R	A	S	E			
A	V	A		S	E	L	L	S		S	T	R	O	L	L		S	L	A	M
N	I	G	H	T	F	A	L	L		T	R	A	V	E	L	B	O	O	K	S
E	V	E	R		E	R	I	E		E	I	N	E	R		O	P	T	I	C
W	A	D	S		R	O	S	S		D	O	G	S		A	S	S	N	S	

#49

A	D	Z	E		C	H	A	R	T		S	L	A	T		O	B	J	E	T
L	A	O	N		R	O	G	E	R		N	O	V	I		R	O	A	M	S
A	C	O	W		E	R	O	D	E		O	R	I	N		P	R	I	M	A
I	H	I	R	E	D	A	N	O	X	F	O	R	D	S	C	H	O	L	A	R
	A	D	E	L	I	E			E	T	E		M	E	A	N				
		A	I	T		M	A	R	R	Y		K	I	L	N		O	F	F	
K	E	A	T	S		M	A	D	A	M		M	I	T	E		F	L	O	E
Y	E	S	H	E	H	A	D	A	N	I	R	I	S	H	B	R	O	G	U	E
A	R	T	E		A	L	E	R	T		E	L	S			E	X	A	L	T
C	I	E		A	D	A		M	A	N	E		O	D	E					
K	E	P	T	S	A	Y	I	N	G	B	L	E	S	S	M	Y	S	O	L	E
			R	A	T		N	O	R	A		W	E	E		W	E	S		
A	G	A	I	N		S	T	U		W	A	K	E	N		S	N	I	T	
J	U	S	T	A	S	S	T	U	B	B	O	R	N	A	S	A	M	U	L	E
A	N	T	E		W	E	E	P		A	R	M	O	R		P	A	P	A	S
R	K	O		H	E	A	P		B	R	E	S	T		I	A	L			
	H	A	L	L		C	O	G				U	N	C	L	A	D			
F	I	N	A	L	L	Y	G	A	V	E	H	I	M	T	H	E	B	O	O	T
E	X	U	L	T		H	A	R	I		A	N	I	T	A		E	R	T	E
T	I	T	L	E		A	M	E	N		M	O	R	E	L		E	T	T	A
E	A	S	E	D		M	E	T	E		S	N	O	R	E		R	A	Y	S

#50

D	R	A	P	E	S		A	D	D	E	D↑		S	U	R	M	I	S	E
E	A	T	E	N↑		D	R	I	V	E	R		T	R	A	I	N	E	R
E	N	T	R	A	P		H	E	R	E	T	O		A	N	I	M	A	T	O
P	I	N	E	C	O	N	E	S		R	O	A	S	T		L	E	T↓	S
			T	S	A	R	S		S	O	R	T	I	E	S				
L	I	E↓		E	Y	E	S			R	O	M	A		C	A	B		
A	R	M	L	E	S	S		U	S	E↑		I	N	S	T	A	N	C	E
R	E	C	O	N		M	I	S	S	T	E	P		D	O	R	A		
K	N	E	A	D		D	O	T	E	S	O	N		S	C	O	T	E	R
S	E	E	D	I	E	S	T		O	W	N↑		H	O	S	E	S↓		
			V	O	T	E	D↓		N	E	W	M	A	N					
F	A	S	T	E	N		L	A	B	S		A	D	M	I	R	A	L	S
U	N	L	E	S	S		R	E	A	D	E	R	S		C	O	R	A	L
E	T	O	N		A	T	A	N	E	N	D		A	L	I	N	E		
L	E	T	T	U	C	E	S		T	E	S	T		C	O	L	L	E	G	E
S↑	S		N	O	N	O				A	S	A	P		↑	S	E	T	
			S	T	A	N	D↑	S		N	I	N	E	R					
G	U	E	S	T		M	E	A	R	A		G	R	E	N	A	D	I	N	E
E	N	D	O	R	S	E		M	O	B	I	L	E		E	V	A	D	E	R
T	O	E	N	A	I	L		P	O	L	L	E	N		D	E	F	E	A	T
↓	S	L	O	P	E	S		S	T	E	E	D	S		↑	S	T	A	T	E

MAKE YOUR PUZZLE COLLECTION COMPLETE
with Simon & Schuster's Convenient Backlist Order Form

Now in its ninth decade of publication.

The Original Crossword Puzzle Series

——0-684-81473-0	#195	Feb. 97	Samson	$9.00
____0-684-86936-5	#218	Feb. 01	Samson	$9.00
____0-684-86937-3	#219	Apr. 01	Samson	$9.95
____0-684-86938-1	#220	Jun. 01	Samson	$9.95
____0-684-86941-1	#222	Oct. 01	Samson	$9.95
____0-7432-0537-5	#223	Dec. 01	Samson	$9.95
____0-7432-5096-6	#236	Feb. 04	Samson	$9.95
____0-7432-5111-3	#237	Apr. 04	Samson	$9.95
____0-7432-5112-1	#238	Jun. 04	Samson	$9.95
____0-7432-5121-0	#239	Aug. 04	Samson	$9.95
____0-7432-5122-9	#240	Oct. 04	Samson	$9.95
____0-7432-5123-7	#241	Dec. 04	Samson	$9.95
____0-7432-5124-5	#242	Feb. 05	Samson	$9.95
____0-7432-5125-3	#243	Apr. 05	Samson	$9.95
____0-7432-5126-1	#244	Jun. 05	Samson	$9.95
____0-7432-5127-X	#245	Aug. 05	Samson	$9.95
____0-7432-5128-8	#246	Oct. 05	Samson	$9.95
____0-7432-5129-6	#247	Dec. 05	Samson	$9.95

Simon & Schuster Crossword Treasuries

——0-684-84366-8	#40	Sept. 99	Samson	$9.00
——0-684-85637-9	S&S 75th Anniversary Vintage Crossword Treasury			
		Apr. 99	Farrar	$9.00
____0-7432-4795-7	#41	Nov. 03	Samson/Maleska	$10.00

Simon & Schuster Crostics

——0-671-87193-5	#111	July 94	Middleton	$8.00
——0-684-81380-7	#114	Nov. 95	Middleton	$8.00
——0-684-82963-0	#116	Nov. 96	Middleton	$8.00
——0-684-83652-1	#117	Aug. 97	Middleton	$8.00

Simon & Schuster Crostics Treasuries

——0-671-87221-4	#3	Mar. 94	Middleton	$8.00
——0-684-84354-4	#5	Mar. 98	Middleton	$9.00
——0-7432-0059-4	#6	Nov. 00	Middleton	$9.00

Simon & Schuster Fun with Crostics Series

——0-684-84277-7	#20	Jan. 98	Duerr	$8.00
——0-684-84361-7	#21	Jun. 98	Duerr	$8.00
——0-684-85942-4	#24	July 99	Duerr	$8.00

Simon & Schuster Super Crostics Books

——0-671-51132-7	#3	Mar. 95	Middleton	$10.00
——0-684-81340-8	#4	Mar. 97	Middleton	$10.00
——0-684-84364-1	#5	Mar. 99	Middleton	$10.00

Simon & Schuster Super Crossword Books

——0-671-79232-6	#7	Nov. 92	Maleska	$10.00
——0-671-89709-8	#8	Nov. 94	Maleska	$10.00
——0-684-82964-9	#9	Nov. 96	Maleska	$10.00
——0-684-84365-X	#10	Oct. 98	Samson	$10.00
____0-684-87186-6	#11	May 01	Samson	$10.00
——0-7432-5538-0	#12	Nov. 04	Samson/Maleska	$10.00

Simon & Schuster Large Type Crossword Puzzle Books

——0-684-81187-1	#1	Oct. 95	Maleska	$10.00
——0-684-84367-6	#3	Nov. 99	Maleska	$9.00

Savage Crossword Puzzle Series

——0-684-87195-5	#1	Jul. 00	Savage	$12.00
____0-684-87196-3	#2	Mar. 01	Savage	$12.00

S&S Super Crossword Puzzle Dictionary and Reference Book

——0-684-85696-4		Apr. 99	$15.00

SEND ORDERS TO:

**Simon & Schuster Inc.
Order Processing
Department**

**100 Front Street
Riverside, NJ 08075
Customer Service:
1-800-223-2336
Fax: 1-800-943-9831**

Total Cost of All Books Ordered _____

Add Applicable State Sales Tax _____

Check or Money Order Enclosed for _____

Please Charge VISA ____ MASTERCARD ____ AMEX ____

Card # _____ Exp. Date _____

Signature _____

Ship to:

Name _____

Address _____

City _____ State _____ Zip Code _____

PLEASE NOTE:
Prices subject to change without prior notice. If any part of your order is out of stock when we receive it, we will ship available titles and will send a refund for the portion we cannot fill.

FIRESIDE
A Division of Simon & Schuster
A VIACOM COMPANY

Printed in the United States
By Bookmasters